Math in Minutes

Math in Minutes

Easy
Activities
for Children
Ages 4-8

Sharon
MacDonald

gryphon house

Silver Spring, Maryland

Bulk purchase

Gryphon House books are available for special premiums and sales promotions as well as for fund-raising use. Special editions or book excerpts also can be created to specification. For details, contact the Director of Marketing at Gryphon House.

Disclaimer

Gryphon House, Inc. and the author cannot be held responsible for damage, mishap, or injury incurred during the use of or because of activities in this book.

Appropriate and reasonable caution and adult supervision of children involved in activities and corresponding to the age and capability of each child involved, is recommended at all times. Do not leave children unattended at any time. Observe safety and caution at all times.

Every effort has been made to locate copyright and permission information.

©2007 Sharon MacDonald
Printed in the United States of America.

Published by Gryphon House, Inc.
10770 Columbia Pike, Suite 201, Silver Spring, MD 20901
301.595.9500; 301.595.0051 (fax); 800.638.0928 (toll-free)

Visit us on the web at www.gryphonhouse.com

Illustrations by Deborah C. Johnson

Reprinted April 2010

Library of Congress Cataloging-in-Publication Data

MacDonald, Sharon, 1942-
  Math in minutes / Sharon MacDonald ; illustrations by Deborah C. Johnson.
      p. cm.
  Includes index.
  ISBN 978-0-87659-057-7
  1. Mathematics--Study and teaching (Primary)--Activity programs. I. Title.
  QA135.6.M33 2007
  372.7--dc22

                              2007004511

Table of Contents

CHAPTER 4

Measurement, Seriation, Time, and Money 53

CHAPTER 5

Geometry and Spatial Sense 79

CHAPTER 6

Sorting, Classifying, Graphing, Data Analysis, and Probability 99

CHAPTER 7

Patterns and Number Relationships 117

CHAPTER 8

Problem Solving and Reasoning 133

Teach Math? Me?

CHAPTER 1

I never liked math, and that is why I wanted to write this book. I was an active child and math was hard for me. Frankly, it often made me feel stupid, overwhelmed, and frustrated. Throughout years of teaching, I learned many teachers share my feelings.

When I first became an early childhood teacher, I worried that my principal would find out about my math skills and conclude that I wasn't able to teach math to the children. I was afraid that I might even lose my job! Then Cammi came into my class, and she changed my life and my outlook about math.

Cammi loved rocks. Every day, she brought in a handful of them to share with the class. We measured, sorted, weighed, counted, and graphed her rocks during morning Group Time. It was a smash hit. As time passed, the other children's interest in the rocks waned, but Cammi continued to bring her rocks in, day after day, one handful at a time. Eventually, one day, I decided to let Cammi do independent rock projects while the rest of the children were in the usual morning Group Time activities. Cammi would work with her rocks in the Math Center, I thought, and report her findings to the entire group later.

In the Math Center, Cammi had several options for activities to do with her rocks. There was a blank Venn diagram, a blank graph, number lines, several sorting trays, and a roll of adding machine tape hung from a cup hook (for measuring the lengths of things).

While the rest of the class was in Group Time, I kept an eye on Cammi. She worked in the Math Center all morning. When Group Time ended for the rest of the children and they transitioned to different centers, Cammi yelled, "If anyone needs a number line they can use mine." I went over to see what she had done. Evidently, Cammi could not find the basket of number lines, so she made one of her own.

Cammi wrote ascending numbers on a strip of adding machine tape, and placed a rock on each different number as a way to count them. Cammi learned that "7" was the total of the rocks, and she counted them rationally.

Wow! I was impressed.

Teaching Math

Using rocks as a tool to teach math worked for Cammi because she was interested in rocks. Cammi learned new math skills and met important academic goals because she liked the materials. Establishing such interest engages children's natural curiosity, which can lead to learning in the way it did for Cammi. Cammi taught me that for young children, math is not desk work. For math to make sense to young children, it needs to relate to everyday events happening in their lives. Most of our days are full of mathematical problems children can solve.

Rational counting means attaching numbers in order to a series of objects in a group, just as Cammi was doing with the rocks. Rote counting, on the other hand, is when a child recites the order of numbers from memory: "One, two, three, four, five, six, seven, eight, nine, 10."

Doodling

Although doodling is not part of math, it helps people relax and find solutions to problems. The brain likes to doodle because when you use your thumb and fingers to manipulate a pencil, it requires about one third of the brain's processing power, which really lights up the brain's circuitry. The next time you need to solve a problem, pick up a pencil—it is the fastest way to link your creativity to your mental crunching power!

What Is Math?

What is **math** anyway? Math is about relationships—the relationships between numbers, events, objects, systems, and cycles; it is, of course, about calculating; and it is also about figuring things out in an organized way.

Cammi learned several things during this activity:

- that a number line is a tool;
- how to perform one-to-one correspondence and rational counting;
- that numbers ascend on the number line, from left to right; and
- how to write the numerals 1–7.

Cammi also met National Council of Teachers of Mathematics (NCTM) curriculum goals for early childhood students by learning to:

- value mathematics;
- become confident in her math ability;
- become a mathematical problem-solver;
- communicate mathematically using numbers, symbols, and words; and
- reason mathematically.

Cammi met each of these curriculum goals on her own by playing and exploring with her rocks.

Below is an example of how to pose simple, mathematical problems for children as well as provide them with an interactive way to use mathematical tools to solve the problems. It takes just a few minutes, and it is a good illustration of what children can do with a little teacher direction. They can solve the problem!

1. **What's the problem (question)?**
   "How many apples do we need for snack? Each person can have half an apple."
2. **How will we find the answer?**
   "Maybe what we need to do is put the two people who are going to share an apple together. What do you think?"
3. **How will we execute the plan?**
   "Should we count the apples that are going to be shared?"
4. **What is the result?**
   "How many apples? Eleven?"

This example poses an everyday mathematical problem and includes the intermediate steps that allow the children to reach the solution. It may take more time and thought than a simple addition problem, but it is worth the investment of both.

The intermediate steps are easy to leave out, because adults do them in their heads. But verbalizing these steps makes it easier for children to figure out the answer by themselves. The above example uses steps 1 *through* 4, not 1 *then* 4.

Literacy and No Child Left Behind (NCLB)

With the NCLB emphasis on reading, writing, speaking, listening, and testing, I knew I needed quick and easy-to-use math lessons to cover the math standards. I wanted the children to be excited about math, too, and develop their skills. I decided that the only way for me to approach it was to build math standards into the small events and activities that took place in the classroom during the day. Here is what I did:

1. I posted a list of the NCTM math standards in (see appendix pages 186 and 187) the Math Center. I also kept a copy in my lesson plan book.

2. I reviewed the ages and stages of math development so I could knowledgeably observe what changes were happening for each child and what to expect as the children developed skills (see Stages of Math Development below).

3. Based on my observations, I found ways to use daily classroom activities to teach math.

4. I incorporated the NCTM standards into my math curriculum.

Stage One
(two to three years old)

Children:
- use numbers as they hear other people using them;
- actively explore objects and games like large-piece puzzles;
- use direction and relational words like *on* and *off*, *here* and *there*, and *up* and *down*;
- recognize a circle; and
- sequence up to three items.

Stage Two
(three to four years old)

Children:
- recognize and express quantities using words like *some*, *more*, *a lot*, and *another*;
- reveal an emerging sense of time;
- recognize geometric shapes in the environment;
- sort objects by one characteristic;
- rote count to five;
- notice and compare similarities and differences;
- recognize simple patterns; and
- use words to describe quantities and sizes, like *short*, *long*, *tall*, *a lot*, *a little*, and *big*.

Stage Three
(four to five years old)

Children:

- play number games with understanding;
- count objects from 1–10, or 1–20;
- identify the larger of two numbers;
- answer simple questions that require logic;
- understand one-to-one correspondence up to 10;
- recognize a penny and a nickel;
- combine whole numbers up to 10;
- make estimates and predictions in real life situations;
- recognize more complex patterns;
- use position words;
- sort forms by shape;
- sort objects by one or two attributes;
- identify a circle, square, triangle, and rectangle;
- compare the sizes of familiar objects not in sight; and
- work multi-piece puzzles.

Stage Four
(five to six years old)

Children:

- understand concepts represented in symbolic form;
- combine simple sets;
- begin to add small numbers in their heads;
- rote count to 100 with little confusion;
- count objects to 20 and higher;
- understand that numbers are symbols for the totals of concrete things;
- understand one-to-one correspondence;
- recognize that two parts make a whole;
- count by fives and 10s to 100;
- count backwards from 10;
- use nonstandard and standard measuring tools;
- recognize, describe, extend, and create a variety of patterns;
- use patterns to predict what comes next;
- sort and classify real objects or pictures by multiple attributes; and
- decide which number comes before and after an object number.

This book offers fun, simple activities you can do with children using materials you already have in your classroom. You will still have structured math time to teach math skills, as the need arises naturally, such as writing the number of letters in their names or creating timelines to track a plant's growth, but the practical application will come throughout the day when you apply math concepts to everyday activities.

Math and Literacy

Math helps build literacy skills, and it is easier than you may think to put math and literacy together. Math offers several new words with which the children can expand their vocabularies, from simple words like *small, yesterday, first, same, far away*, and *square*, to more math-specific terms such as those listed below. Use the vocabulary with the children. Come up with a math alphabet of your own and post it on a classroom wall to remind the children to use the words. Add new words to the list as they emerge from everyday math experiences (see The Math Alphabet below).

A = adding

B = bar graph

C = circumference

D = degrees

E = estimation

F = fraction

G = graph

H = hundred

I = inch

J = justify

K = kilogram

L = line

M = money

N = numeral

O = one

P = pattern

Q = quarter

R = ruler

S = subtraction

T = tally

U = unit

V = Venn diagram

W = weight

X = X-axis

Y = yesterday

Z = zero

Math Standards

National Council of Teachers of Mathematics (NCTM) standards stress three literacy areas: communication, connections, and reasoning.

Communication means that the children use math words to describe ideas. For example: *two, less, small, yesterday, long, first, more, at, same, in, square, far away, old, big, how many?, when?, time, day, faster, bunch,* and *measure.*

Making connections means that the children use the math skills and math words they have learned in other classroom topics and in their daily living. Some examples are:

- measuring plant growth while doing a science project;
- estimating the number of raisins in their cups at snack time;
- working a puzzle with 10 pieces;
- bouncing a ball 10 times while playing outside;
- reading a counting book;
- comparing the sizes of shoes;
- counting how many people can play Concentration;
- finding a square piece to fit in a box;
- putting the collage pieces *above, below,* or *beside* each other; and
- using play money at a pretend grocery store.

Reasoning means that the children can draw conclusions from a given set of facts or circumstances and that they can explain events and the methods and techniques used to compile and communicate information. Informally, they can make observations using thought processes such as, "If I want to know this, I do that," and, "I show it to others like this because it is the best way among the choices available."

Here are some examples of independent activities done by different children in a classroom setting, which show their reasoning skills:

Situation: Ask the child to make a leaf graph, and explain what the leaf graph means.
Child's report: "There is only one pointy leaf, five round ones, and eight long, skinny ones."

Situation: Ask the child to draw a box around different numbers with similar characteristics and explain why.
Child's report: "I put the box around the 1, 4, and 7 because they look like they are made with sticks like the 'k' and 't.' I put the box around the 2, 6, and 9 because they have curves. I put the box around 3 and 5 because they have bumps."

Situation: Ask the child to measure his friend's height.
Child's solution: He asks his friend to lie down on the floor, and then puts down blocks end to end from his friend's head to his toe. They count the blocks.

While traveling and presenting at workshops and conferences throughout the United States, I have talked to teachers about what they do to teach math while adhering to NCLB program guidelines. Frequently, teachers say that although they spend lots of time creating math activities, the children finish them in two minutes. That is not much of a return on the time they invest in the activities. Many activities that the teachers create are right-answered, meaning activities that have one single answer or solution, in the same way that a puzzle is **right-answered**. Once the children complete them the first time, the activities are rarely used again. Open-ended activities, on the other hand, offer children the chance to work and rework the activity, and they offer different levels of difficulty for children with different skill levels. With open-ended activities, teachers feel that their time is well invested because the children will use the activity again and again.

Some of the activities in this book are right-answered because children need to build specific skills—tools for them to use throughout their lives. The open-ended, problem-solving activities come later in the book. This is a pattern we see in learning: skill-building activities lead to more open-ended applications of knowledge. We are building a base of learning to be expanded upon later.

Curriculum Focal Points

NCTM recently identified and described three curriculum focal points that help to define instructional goals and learning expectations for mathematics in early childhood. Their intention is to develop a continuing understanding of mathematical competency in all children, including:

1. The use of mathematics to solve problems;
2. The application of logical reasoning to justify procedures and solutions; and
3. The design and analysis of methods used to find answers, use techniques (such as counting, graphing, sorting), and represent information accurately and communicate answers of others.

Chapter 8 of this book, "Problem Solving and Reasoning," deals extensively with examples and activities that incorporate these tasks in the classroom.

How to Use This Book

The chapters of this book correspond to different mathematics objectives. Standards vary from state to state, but the core elements are essentially the same. Look at your own state standards and you will find they generally align with the "Math Objectives That Meet Standards" headings at the beginning of each activity in this book.

The activities are designed to teach a skill, or to review or practice a newly acquired skill. Often, you can use an activity for a child who is ready to work independently or to work at a slightly higher level. Many of the activities, for example, can be placed in the Math Center for independent work. When one activity can be used in different ways depending on the needs of individual children, it is easier for the teacher to differentiate instruction for children in one class who are working at different skill levels.

The activities in each chapter are in order from easiest to most difficult. Any activity, however, can be made more challenging or easier depending on how you use it with a particular child.

In the back of this book, you will find a matrix of the NCTM Standards for Pre-Kindergarten Through Second Grade. Each activity in this book meets NCTM objectives for mathematics, but the phrasing in this book is more similar to state standards than that of NCTM standards. They correspond to the math skill expectations for the children you teach. For more information on detailed instructional programs and standards in mathematics, visit the NCTM Web site at www.nctm.org.

Where do you begin? I suggest that you begin with ideas that build on math activities you already do with your children, and proceed from there. This book is a basic introduction to early childhood math. It introduces teachers, college students, assistant teachers, and parents to the basic math concepts young children need to learn.

You will find ways to make activities more challenging for children by using the **Take It Up a Level** sections in each chapter. **In Addition** broadens the topics in interesting ways and shows how to understand math in a different way or provide information about a topic related to math. **Count on This** contains helpful information that I used throughout my teaching career. It is part philosophy, part psychology, and all sound teaching practice. It all helped me. Maybe it will do the same for you.

A list of helpful resources is at the end of the book.

Number Sense and Numeration

CHAPTER 2

What Is ...?

A **number** is a symbol for a unit of one or more things. Another word for number is *numeral*. The word *numeral* describes the written version of a number. For example: "There were 11 people on the island" ("11" in this case is a numeral). However, when writing about numerals, they are called *numbers*. For example, "Eleven is the *number* of people on the island."

What Is ...?

Number sense is the awareness that numbers help us organize our day-to-day lives to accomplish the things we want to do. It is always better, for instance, to have two shoes—one for each foot—when you get dressed for school, and two cookies, rather than one, especially if you are hungry at snack.

What Is ...?

Numeration is just a big word for counting.

The Developmental Levels of Counting

There are developmental levels to counting. If we observe what young children do at different ages, and we know what to look for, we can find out how effectively they are acquiring new math skills. Understanding the typical developmental levels for children of different ages provides some sense of what it is normal to expect a three-year-old to be able to do as opposed to a five-year-old. Also, such awareness helps teachers recognize potential developmental problems before they impact later learning.

Level 1 (two to three years)
The child moves objects around randomly. No effort is made, for instance, to sort, sequence, or organize them by some mental notion or organizing plan held by the child. In the Block Center, for example, I asked Justin, "Wow, how many blocks did you use to make that structure?" He pointed and smiled, touched some of the blocks, but not all of them.

Level 2 (three to four years)
When asked a numeration question, children make rough guesses. For example, a child may count: "1, 5, 10, 22, 7, 100." Similarly, I once

asked a child, "How old do you think I am?" "Oh," said Jeremy, "You are not too old... about, maybe 153."

I never asked Jeremy to guess (estimate) my age again.

Level 3 (four to six years)

Children use one-to-one correspondence to problem-solve. For example, as she was setting the table in the Home Living Center, Sarah said, "Jason gets one plate, Susie gets one plate, A.J. gets one plate, and I get one plate. That's one, two, three, four plates." Sarah was doing *informal, rational counting*. Rational counting means attaching numbers in order to a series of objects in a group as compared to rote counting, on the other hand, which is when a child recites the order of numbers from memory: "One, two, three, four, five, six, seven, eight, nine, 10."

Level 4 (five to seven years)

Children count equal numbers in separate groups of items. For example, LaKeisha said, "I have 15 buttons, now I need 15 sticky dots." She counts the 15 buttons and 15 sticky dots. She puts the 15 sticky dots on a sheet of paper and then glues the 15 buttons on top of each dot.

The developmental levels of counting were adapted from the following sources:

Schiller, P. (1997). *Practices in the Early Childhood Classroom (The DLM Early Childhood Professional Library 1)*. Worthington, OH: SRA/Macmillan/McGraw-Hill.

Miller, K. (2001). *Ages and Stages Revised*. West Palm Beach, FL: Telshare Publishing Co., Inc.

Charlesworth, R. and K.K. Lind. (1995). *Math and Science for Young Children, 2nd edition*. Albany, NY: Delmar Publishers.

NAEYC and NCTM Standards

The information in these books was filtered through my own personal experiences and observations as a teacher and a trainer of teachers to arrive at the format I present in this book.

Activities That Teach Number Sense and Numeration

"Leaves Are Falling"

Materials

10 leaves
number line (with numbers 2' apart),
  or number squares numbered
  1–10 drawn with chalk

Count on This

Start a rainy-day activities bucket. Collect artificial leaves and put them in the bucket along with other activities you can do inside on rainy days.

In Addition

Children will love it if you take a brightly colored umbrella outside when the leaves are falling. Open it with a flourish, and ask the children to follow the umbrella as they search for leaves.

Math Objectives That Meet Standards

Children will:
1. Count by multiples of 1, 2, 5, and 10.
2. Practice one-to-one correspondence.

Leaves Are Falling
Tune: Are You Sleeping?
(from the *Watermelon Pie and Other Tunes* CD by Sharon MacDonald)

Leaves are falling,
One, two, three,
From the tree.
Four, five, six,
Falling to the ground.
Seven, eight, nine,
Ten leaves falling down,
Covering the ground.

How to Do It

- This song teaches numeration and number sense. All you need is children and leaves!
- Bring the children outside. Choose 10 children and ask them to collect one leaf each from the ground (if no leaves are available, use construction paper cutouts).
- When the children have their leaves, ask them to put the leaves together in a pile, counting in order as they place them in the pile, so they understand that the pile contains 10 leaves.
- After making the pile, ask the children to pick up their leaves and stand on one of the numbers on the number line.
- Ask them to count off, 1–10, so it is clear each child knows the number on which she is standing.
- Together with all the children, sing "Leaves Are Falling," having each child drop her leaf when the children say the number on which she is standing.

Take It Up a Level

When the children are ready for something more difficult, change the words of the song to count by multiples of 2, 5, or 10 and sing it again.

"Leaves Are Falling" Interactive Chart

Materials

eight sentence strips
30 index cards
markers
basket
pocket chart

Count on This

Offer variations of the activity with different levels of difficulty, so children can succeed according to their abilities. Children will begin working where they are most comfortable, and as they experience success, will likely move on to more difficult activities. Successful experiences will lead to more children taking on greater challenges.

Math Objectives That Meet Standards

Children will:
1. Recognize numbers.
2. Match numbers to number words.
3. Match number words to number words.
4. Identify the number of objects the number represents.
5. Understand that numbers always represent the same quantity.
6. Practice one-to-one correspondence.

How to Do It

- Set up this activity in the Interactive Chart Center or Music Center.
- Write each line of "Leaves Are Falling" (see the previous page) on one of eight sentence strips and put the sentence strips in a pocket chart.
- Write the number words (*one, two, three,* and so on), the numerals (*1, 2, 3,* and so on), drawings of the number of leaves (one leaf on one card, two leaves on the second card, and so on), and the number of leaves in words (*one leaf, two leaves, three leaves,* and so on) on index cards and put them in a basket next to the pocket chart.
- Challenge the children to match the different versions of the numbers with one another. (Matching each different version of a number presents its own level of difficulty.) For example, the children can match a numeral to its number word, match a number word to the same number word of leaves, match the numbered leaf drawing to its number word, and so on.
- After the children master the activity at this level, remove the sentence strips from the chart and put them in the basket without the cards.
- Challenge the children to put the song back together in its proper order.

Take It Up a Level

As the children become more proficient at this activity, challenge them to count by multiples of 2, 5, and 10.

What Is ...?

Interactive means that the children do something with the materials; they are involved directly, hands on, with the activity.

Number Bag

Materials

10 brown paper lunch bags
marker
number line (use adding machine
tape and write the numbers 1–10;
write each number 4' apart on the
adding machine strip)

Count on This

Young children are short on patience,
so explain that they will each have a
turn to do this activity. Put up a
checklist that shows which children
have had a turn and which children
will be next. If a child asks when her
turn will be, refer her to the list.
This will free up your teaching time!

Math Objectives That Meet Standards

Children will:
1. Recognize that any number is a symbol for a collection of objects
   that can be counted individually. For example, "4" represents the
   total of four objects that one can count or accept as true.
2. Practice one-to-one correspondence.
3. Compare numbers of objects.

How to Do It

- Write the numbers 1–10 on the front of separate bags.
- On the back of each bag, draw the same number of dots (for
  example: two dots on the bag marked 2, six dots on the bag
  marked 6).
- At different times of the day, challenge groups of 10 children to
  each select one of the bags, and then, as they go through the day,
  put the correct number of objects in each bag (for example, a
  child might put five crayons in the number 5 bag).
- If a particular child does not recognize the number on her bag, let
  her ask a friend for help identifying the number.
- Encourage the children who have difficulty associating the
  numerals with the amounts they signify to use the dots on the
  bags for one-to-one correspondence, matching each of the objects
  they put in their bags to one of the dots on the back of the bags.
- Set out the number line.
- When the children finish filling the bags, have them put their bags
  on the correct numbers, then move to another activity.
- From time to time, grab a bag and ask, "Who filled the number 5
  bag?" The child who filled it will come to you right away! Ask her
  to count the objects for you. You can do this during Group Time,
  but I suggest doing it individually with each child so you can
  better assess what each child knows.
- It may take a few days for all of the children to count the objects
  in their bags.

Take It Up a Level

Replace the numbers with number words on each bag (for example,
"five" replaces "5"), and send the children looking for things to put
in the bags.

What Is …?

Numerical inclusion refers to the *total* number of children. For
example, you are practicing numerical inclusion when you say "five
children," rather than "fifth child." So, when you say, "I am with five
children," that is a bunch. Saying you are "with the fifth child," on
the other hand, means that you are with one—which is not much of a
bunch!

Numeral/ Number Bag Match

Materials

10 brown paper lunch bags
counting objects, such as pebbles,
buttons, or paper clips
notebook ring

Count on This

Children relate well to simple truths. For example: "If the bottom falls out of my lunch bag, what's inside is too heavy!" Children learn some things best through experiencing them. As long as a child is not at risk, let her have the experience!

Math Objectives That Meet Standards

Children will:
1. Practice one-to-one correspondence.
2. Recognize numbers 1–10.
3. Read number words *one* through *ten*.
4. Understand that a number is the total of objects that the number represents.

How to Do It

- Write the number *1* on the bottom of a bag and write the word *one* on the front of the bag.
- Fold the bag's bottom flap over, exposing the paper beneath the fold, and draw one dot. (See illustration below.)
- Repeat this with all 10 bags, increasing the numeral, the number word, and the number of dots by one each time.
- Punch a hole in the upper left-hand corner of the flap of each bag, and attach the notebook ring.
- Encourage the children to put the correct number of counting objects in each bag.

Calendar Collage

Materials

old calendars
scissors
glue sticks
9" x 12" pieces of construction paper

Math Objectives That Meet Standards

Children will:
1. Count and identify the numbers 1–31.
2. Recognize that a number represents a quantity.

How to Do It

- Do this collage activity in the Art Center.
- Put calendar pages in a basket with scissors, paper, and glue sticks.
- Invite the children to cut out the calendar squares and glue them to a piece of construction paper. Tell them they don't have to cut out one square each time. They can cut out several squares, or cut the squares in different shapes.
- Encourage the children to cover the entire piece of paper with number squares cut out from the calendars. It is freeform fun! The children love to do it and it helps develop fine motor skills.
- Display the collages on the wall at eye level.
- Whenever you have a few minutes, ask a child to read the numbers on her collage.

Count on This

Children love calendars simply because you and other important adults in their lives work with them. Use yours every day. (Start the mornings by asking the children, "What day is it?")

Take It Up a Level

When the children's collages are dry, ask them to write the number words for as many of the numbers on their collages as they are able.

In Addition

Toward the end of the calendar year, go to stores that sell calendars. Ask them to donate their last year's calendars to your classroom. Try to get there before they send the calendars back to the manufacturers.

What Is ...?

A **collage** is an assembly of pieces of paper or fabric usually glued to the surface of a heavy paper or board called a *base*.

Number Rings

Materials

three to four notebook rings
three to four sets of 10 index cards
sticky dots

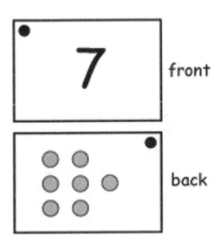

front

back

Math Objectives That Meet Standards

Children will:
1. Recognize numerals 1–10.
2. Count numbers from to 1–10.
3. Practice one-to-one correspondence.

How to Do It

- Do this activity in the Math Center.
- Write the numbers 1–10 on 10 index cards, one number per card.
- Put the same number of stickers on the back of each card (for example, put nine stickers on the back of the number 9 card).
- Punch a hole in one corner of each card and loop a notebook ring through the holes. (See illustration.)
- Invite the children to use the ring to count forward or backward. Also, they can match items to the numbers, or match objects to the dots on the back of the index cards.
- Make 2–3 number rings. Use the index cards for counting by multiples, too.
- You can also extend the number range to 20, or even higher, depending on the children's skill levels.

Balloon Launch

Materials

hot dog-shaped balloon
drinking straw
15'–20' length of string
tape

Count on This

Explain and review skills with demonstrations or pictures. It will reduce your teaching time by almost half.

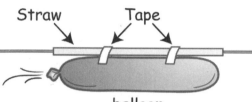

Straw   Tape

balloon

Math Objectives That Meet Standards

Children will:
1. Count backward from 10–1.

How to Do It

- Attach a string diagonally, wall-to-wall, across the corner of the classroom, above the heads of the children, slipping the straw onto one end of the string before attaching that end to the wall.
- Blow up the balloon and pinch it closed. Ask a child to tape the balloon to the straw, from one side of the balloon to the other (see illustration).
- With the children, count down from 10–1, and then release the pinched end of the balloon.
- Watch the balloon fly across the corner of the room on the string. This is one of the most popular activities in my classroom, so be prepared to do it whenever you have a few minutes on your hands.

Safety Note: Keep the balloon out of the children's reach. If the balloon pops, make sure to pick up all the pieces. Uninflated balloons and pieces of balloons pose a choking hazard.

In Addition

Keep an old TV remote control unit handy so children can enter numbers while waiting for the balloon to launch.

Number Bracelets

Materials

10 empty cardboard masking tape rolls
colored masking tape or contact paper
sticky dots

Count on This

Recycling saves you money. You can use the savings to buy something you cannot recycle or make.

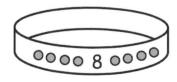

Math Objectives That Meet Standards

Children will:
1. Recognize and put numbers 1–10 in numerical order.
2. Recognize and identify numerals.
3. Count from 1–10 aloud.

How to Do It

- Set up this activity in the Math Center.
- Wrap 10 empty cardboard masking tape rolls with colored masking tape or cover them with contact paper.
- Write the numbers 1–10 on the rolls, one number per roll.
- Attach the same number of sticky dots on the opposite side of each roll.
- Encourage the children to put the "number bracelets" on their arms in numerical order (see illustration).

In Addition

FedEx and UPS locations use a lot of packing tape. Take an empty box to one of these locations and ask them to fill it with their empty rolls. It won't take long for you to have enough to do this activity.

I Spy Numbers Book

Materials

magazines and a newspaper
advertising section, in color
scissors
six 9" x 12" sheets of construction
  paper

Count on This

When children do something
themselves, they are "invested" in it,
and are more likely to remember
what they learned.

Math Objectives That Meet Standards

Children will:
1. Count objects aloud.
2. Recognize numbers.

How to Do It

○ Before doing this activity, hold a piece of paper vertically (the "tall" way) and draw a 2" x 2" square in the upper left hand corner of five sheets of paper.

○ Write the numbers 1–5 in the squares, one number per page (the sixth sheet will be the book cover). Photocopy the pages so each child will have a page.

○ As a group, help and encourage the children to cut out numerals and pictures from magazine and newspaper ads indicating certain numbers of objects (1–5), and organize them into piles, one for each number.

○ Divide the children into groups of five. Give each group six pages (the numbered pages and book cover page). Each child makes a numeral collage on one page of the book, composed of pictures they like and pictures with numerals on them, gluing the corresponding numeral cutouts and pictures to her sheet of paper. As they create each page of the book, challenge the children to "hide" the pictures of numerals among the other pictures on their pages.

○ Let all the pages dry.

○ Encourage each group to help design the cover for their book.

○ When done, staple the pages of each book together and put them in the Math or Library Center. These *I Spy* books often become very popular in the classroom because the children love to read and review their own work. The title (cover) of the books is "I Spy Numbers." The children read the book by looking at the numeral in the upper left hand corner (for example 2) and then finding all the 2s on the page. They say "I spy a 2" and point to the numeral each time they see it.

Take It Up a Level

Encourage the children to find pictures and numerals in magazines and newspaper ads, and each make their own books. If the children are able, challenge them to make collage books with up to 10 or 20 pages.

Number Bottle

Materials

empty plastic soda bottle, any size
sand
two sets of 1–10 number beads
seashells, round beads, pebbles, and
  stars
hot glue gun (for adult use only)
  and glue stick
small plastic bowl
child-safe plastic tweezers
adding machine tape
laminator

In Addition

If you don't have sand, use confetti.
Add small foil numbers rather than
number beads (number beads will
fall to the bottom of a bottle of
confetti because of their weight).

Math Objectives That Meet Standards

Children will:
1. Count objects aloud from 1–10.
2. Select and match numbers 1–10.
3. Recognize numbers.

How to Do It

- Wash and dry the soda bottle. Fill it ¾ full of sand.
- Add one set of 1–10 number beads, and then add seashells, round beads, pebbles, and stars. Twist the cap back on and test the bottle by shaking it, making sure that the number beads are visible. Glue the top with a hot glue gun (adults only).
- Put the second set of number beads in a small plastic bowl, along with a set of child-safe tweezers.
- Make a number line by writing the numerals 1–10 on a piece of adding machine tape about 18"–24" long, and laminate it for durability.
- Place the number bottle and number line in the Math Center.
- Invite the children to take turns shaking the bottle and looking for a number.
- When a child sees a number (8, for example), ask her to find the matching number 8 bead in the small container and pick it up with the tweezers, then match the bead to the 8 on the number line.
- This activity is great for developing the children's fine motor skills.

Before-and-After Calendar Days

Materials

Group Time calendar
Post-it notes that fit within the
  squares on the Group Time
  calendar

Math Objectives That Meet Standards

Children will:
1. Recognize and put numbers 1–10 in numerical order.
2. Identify numbers coming before and after an object number.

How to Do It

- During Group Time, bring out the calendar, and put a Post-it note over one of the date squares on the calendar, the 6th, for example.
- Ask the children, "What number comes after 5 and before 7?"
- Choose a child to come up to the calendar and write the answer on the Post-it note.
- After she finishes, lift the Post-it note to see if the answer matches.
- Do this with any number, 1–31.

Take It Up a Level

Use the Post-it notes to cover a connected sequence of numbers (such as 6, 7, 8). Ask the children to recite the other numbers aloud, and say which numbers are covered.

An **object number** on the calendar is the day the teacher wants to highlight with the activity. In this activity, "6" is the object number because the children are asked, "What comes after 5 and before 7?"

Pompom Counting

Materials

10 clear 5-ounce or 7-ounce plastic cups
black marker
4' length of clothesline
cup hooks or removable adhesive hooks
10 large clothespins
55 pompoms

Math Objectives That Meet Standards

Children will:
1. Count objects aloud from 1–10.
2. Practice one-to-one correspondence.
3. Match equal numbers of objects to written numbers.

How to Do It

- Use a low-traffic corner of the room to set up this activity.
- Write the numbers 1–10 on the clear plastic cups with a black marker, so each cup has one number.
- On the opposing walls of the corner, and at a height that the children can reach, put up the clothesline using cup hooks or removable adhesive hooks.
- Put the cups and pompoms in a basket under the clothesline (see illustration).
- Challenge the children to clip the plastic cups in correct numerical order on the clothesline using clothespins to anchor the cups.
- Further challenge the children by asking them to put the correct number of pompoms in each cup. Explain to the children as they are counting the pompoms that the last number they count will be the total number of pompoms for that cup.

In Addition

The unusual gets attention! Using clothespins and a clothesline is more fun and exciting than just having the cups lined up on a table. The children will be more enthusiastic about this activity.

Pompom-Dot Match

Materials

pompoms of different sizes and
    colors
small container
file folder

Count on This

Color generates enthusiasm. It also accelerates learning. Be colorful! Brain research has shown that color improves the retrieval of information frrom where it is stored. Color is novel, so it attracts the eye to the activity.

Math Objectives That Meet Standards

Children will:

1. Compare a number of objects.
2. Count aloud from 1–10.
3. Select matching numbers.
4. Recognize numbers.

How to Do It

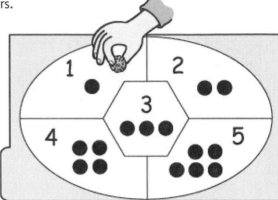

- Open a file folder, and draw several boxes and dots on it, making a game board, as shown in the illustration.
- Place the pompoms in the small container beside the file folder, and invite the children to place the matching number of pompoms on the dots in the correct section of the file folder.

In Addition

Pompoms are inexpensive, and you can do many activities with pompoms. Be sure to have lots of them readily available.

Pompom Toss

Materials

small peel-and-stick numerals
pompoms (one size)
ice tray
small container

Math Objectives That Meet Standards

Children will:

1. Count objects aloud from 1–12.
2. Practice one-to-one correspondence.
3. Understand that a number always represents the same quantity.

How to Do It

- Demonstrate this activity to all the children first, and then move it to the Math Center.
- Attach a peel-and-stick numeral (1–12) to each section of an ice tray, either in numerical order or randomly. (See the illustration.)
- Put the pompoms in a small container.
- Encourage the children to toss pompoms at the tray from a distance of about 2–3'.
- When a pompom lands in one of the tray's cups, challenge the child who threw it to identify the number in that cup.
- Do this until each cup has a pompom in it and the children have identified each number.

Note: If you don't want the children tossing pompoms, provide child-safe tweezers for the children to use to place the pompoms in the cups one at a time, saying the numbers in the cups aloud as they place the pompoms in them.

The Apple Thief

Materials

The Apple Thief by Noreen Cotter
half of an apple for each child

Math Objectives That Meet Standards

Children will:
1. Count aloud from 1–10.
2. Practice one-to-one correspondence.

How to Do It

○ *The Apple Thief* by Noreen Cotter is a great book to read during Snack or Story Time, and is one that the children will want to read with you over and over.

○ Before the children arrive, cut the apples in half and brush lemon juice on their insides to prevent them from turning brown before the children have a chance to eat them.

○ Read *The Apple Thief* to the children.

○ Encourage the children to guess, page by page, what they think is in the tree.

○ Also, on each page, challenge the children to find the worm that is watching the thief.

○ On page seven, where the text talks about taking five nibbles, invite the children to take five nibbles from their apple halves.

○ Continue reading the book and encouraging the children to finish eating their apple halves at the end of the story, when the thief is discovered.

Take It Up a Level

With the children, compose a number story similar to *The Apple Thief*.

Block Cleanup Cards

Materials

blocks
large index cards (4" x 6") or
    cardstock cut to size
markers
large basket

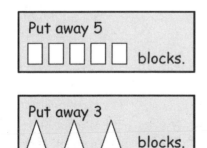

Math Objectives That Meet Standards

Children will:
1. Count objects aloud.
2. Match the number of objects to a number.
3. Recognize numbers.

How to Do It

○ This is a Block Center cleanup activity.

○ Make a variety of "cleanup cards" by writing an instruction and a drawing on each card. For example, write "Put away 5" and draw five of a particular block shape, like a triangular, square, or tubular block (see illustration).

○ Be sure the block shapes exactly match the blocks in the Block Center, as some children will hold blocks up to the cards to see if they match.

○ Place the cards face down in the large basket. Try not to let the children peek at the cards.

○ Invite each child to choose a card, and ask her to follow the directions on the card, picking up the indicated number of the type of block drawn on the card.

Number Playing Cards

Materials

deck of cards (remove the Aces, Kings, Queens, Jacks, and Jokers)
basket
10 3"x 5" index cards

In Addition

Challenge the children to link paper clips, saying aloud the number of each they attach; count buttons, crayons, or days in the year before a major holiday such as Christmas or Thanksgiving; or count rocks or leaves, sorting them based on the different characteristics of each one.

Math Objectives That Meet Standards

Children will:
1. Count objects from 2–10.
2. Match numbers.
3. Recognize numbers.
4. Match numerals to number words.

How to Do It

- Put this activity in the Math or Games and Puzzles Center.
- From a deck of playing cards, separate the cards 2–10 from a single suit (all spades, for example).
- Write the number words for each playing card on separate index cards, and put them in the basket.
- Invite the children to put the playing cards in order from 2–10 (if you have time, talk about the cards that are missing from the deck and why you are not using them).
- When the children have the playing cards in order, challenge them to match the numerals on the cards to the numbers on the index cards.

Coat Hanger Numbers

Materials

index cards
markers
notebook rings
10 wire coat hangers
several dozen clothespins

Count on This

Whenever time permits, challenge the children count from 1–10 and from 10–1.

Math Objectives That Meet Standards

Children will:
1. Practice one-to-one correspondence.
2. Match a number of objects to the same number.
3. Recognize numbers 1–10.

How to Do It

- Write the numbers 1–10 on index cards, one number per card, and attach them to individual coat hangers with notebook rings.
- Hang the coat hangers throughout the room, making sure they are easily within the children's reach.

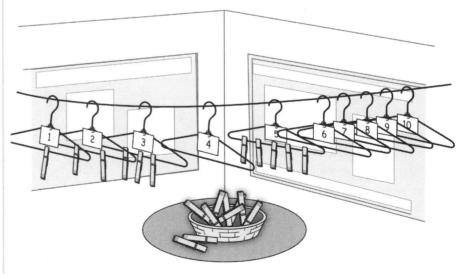

- Place a basket of clothespins in a central location.
- When you have a few minutes, separate the children into groups of three and ask each group to find a particular coat hanger and pin the matching number of clothespins to the coat hanger (for example, if they find the number 5 coat hanger, they would pin five clothespins on it).

Missing Numbers

Materials

plastic or foam oval placemat
permanent marker
10 clothespins

In Addition

You can find plastic and foam placemats at many dollar stores. They are inexpensive to use. Plain oval placemats are a good choice for this activity.

Math Objectives That Meet Standards

Children will:
1. Recognize numerical order 1–20.
2. Identify numbers that are missing from a sequence, and numbers that come before and after a sequence of numbers.
3. Understand and use math vocabulary.

How to Do It

- Set up this activity in the Math Center.
- In permanent marker, write the numbers 1–20 around the edge of the placemat. Omit five or six numbers as you write them, leaving blank the space they would otherwise occupy. (See the illustration.)

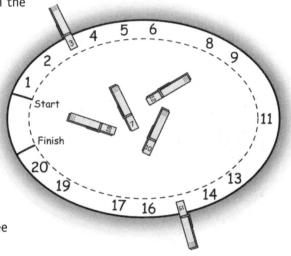

- Write *Start* beside the 1 and *End* beside the 20.
- Write the five or six numbers omitted from the edge of the placemat on the closed ends of clothespins.
- Write several other numbers on clothespins as well, and place all the clothespins in the center of the placemat.
- Invite the children to attach the correct clothespins in the places where there are numbers missing.

What Is ...?

Ordinal Counting describes positions in a series (for example, fifth or sixth). During the day, when an activity arises in which objects or the children are in different ordinal positions, ask the children questions like: "Which/Who came first? Second? Sixth?" "Who is the fifth person in line?" "What comes after first?" "What was the third little pig doing?"

Card Game

Math Objectives That Meet Standards

Children will:
1. Recognize numerals 1–10.
2. Use numbers to describe the number of objects in a set.

Materials

clothesline
playing cards
glue
cardstock
clothespins
basket

How to Do It

- Hang a clothesline between the two walls of a low-traffic corner of the room.
- Remove all the numbered spades from a deck of cards (2–10) and place them in a basket below the clothesline.
- Before the children arrive for the day, attach a few cards to the line using clothespins. For example, put up the 2, 6, and 10, leaving large enough gaps so the cards not yet on the line will fit in order.
- Keep all the leftover spades in the basket.
- Challenge the children to fill in the missing numbers on the line using the cards in the basket.

Take It Up a Level

After the children fill in the missing numbers in the spade suit, change suits to clubs or diamonds. Later, place all the number cards from all the suits in the basket and invite the children to decide which suit to use and put them in order from 2–10 or 10–2.

Ordinal Counting

Math Objectives That Meet Standards

Children will:
1. Use and understand ordinal counting terms such as "first" through "fifth" to describe relative position in a sequence.

Materials

no materials needed

How to Do It

- Do this activity when all the children are in a group together, such as when they are lining up to leave the classroom.
- Ask the children to line up facing into the room (not the door), and challenge them to name the first five children in line, saying, for example, "Sarah is first, Nathan is second, Carrie is third, Ti is fourth, and Casey is fifth."
- Encourage the children to turn around, face the door, and repeat the numbering process. Once they get the order correct, move the children on to the next activity!

Take It Up a Level

Try doing variations on this activity. Ask a group of children, for example, to get in line in order by height, shortest to tallest, and ask them who is first, second, third, fourth, and fifth. Another variation is to ask the children to order themselves based on the dominant colors they are wearing. For example: red is first, blue is second, green is third, yellow is fourth, and white is fifth. Also, challenge the first and third children to bow to each other, then the second and the fourth, and finally, ask the fifth child to bow to the other children.

"Ely and the Five Little Piglets"

Materials

photographs or drawings of piglets

Count on This

Add a rhythmic pattern (sound/silence, short/long) to any text. Beats are patterns. Recognizing patterns is essential to learning to read.

Math Objectives That Meet Standards

Children will:
1. Use the ordinal counting words "first" through "fifth" to describe relative positions in a sequence.
2. Identify *first*, *middle*, and *last* in a series.

How to Do It

⊙ Do this activity when you are lined up in the hall, on the playground, or on the bus on the way to a field trip.
⊙ With the children, chant the following poem. (Chanting adds a rhythmic pattern to the poem, such as a handclap.)
⊙ Show the children the piglet pictures and talk about what piglets eat. Compare them to human babies, so the children understand that piglets need milk, too, until they are ready to eat solid food on their own.

Ely and the Five Little Piglets by Sharon MacDonald
Down in the farm yard, playing around,
Five little piglets rooting in the ground.
The first little pig said, "I want lunch."
The second pig asked for carrots... in a bunch.

The third one said, "I don't want those."
The fourth one snorted, "I'll smell 'em with my nose (snort)."
The fifth one said, "Mama's calling us!"
Pig four suggested that they all ride to Mama's... on the bus?

Pig three sighed, "A bus is silly."
Pig two agreed, "Yeah, silly, really!"
Pig one yelled, "Let's race to the sty."
"No," said Ely, "and I'll tell you why:"

"You could arrive at the sty from the sky, on the sly... if you learned to fly."

Who is this guy Ely?

Ely's the guy who lives near the sty,
Who says that pigs can learn to fly.
Yeah, Ely is the guy who lives near the sty,
Who thinks that pigs can fly when they try.

Now you know Ely.

He is the "you-could-arrive-at-the-sty-from-the-sky, on-the-sly... if-you-learned to-fly" guy.

Take It Up a Level

- For an individual project, give the children sheets of construction paper and several crayons, markers, and so on, and invite them to draw their answers to the question, "Who is Ely?"
- Help the children draw piglet facemasks on paper plates, and then hold them up as they act out the different parts of the poem. (Don't forget, your focus is still on ordinal counting and recognizing relative position.)

Computation and Estimation

CHAPTER 3

What Is ...?

Computation means getting answers using the rules of addition and subtraction. Young children start by counting concrete objects and matching them to a number. By using the rules of computation, children learn that a single operation, like subtraction, answers questions, such as, "If I have three cookies and I eat two of them, how many do I have left?"

Challenge the children to use subtraction to answer "how-many-do-I-have-left-if-I-take-away-this-many" kinds of questions. You can answer other questions put in this way using the same rules.

What Is ...?

Subtraction means deducting one number from another number—you end up with less than you had when you started. Sometimes that is hard for children to accept. For this reason, young children often prefer addition.

What Is ...?

Addition means that you add one number to another. You have more afterward than you had when you started. It is the opposite of subtraction. Almost everyone likes addition.

Learning mathematical operations, like subtraction and addition, shows children that working with numbers is a useful, everyday skill.

Children acquire computation skills through a basic understanding of sets. Sets are groups of things that belong together because they share a common characteristic, such as color or shape. For example, "I have two round red beads and four square green beads. One set of red beads and one set of green beads. If I add the two sets together I have six beads."

From a developmental perspective, as children recognize sets more easily, they are ready to use symbols: plus (+) for addition, minus (−) for subtraction, and the equal sign (=). Essentially, they can write simple math sentences: *(set) A + (set) B =*, and *(set) A − (set) B =*.

What Is ...?

Estimation is making an approximation, or a rough guess, based upon limited information. Estimates are subject to change, as more information about the subject becomes available. When we go to the grocery store, for example, we make a rough guess about how much money we will spend. Let's say we estimate we'll spend $80 for groceries and we spend $76. The estimate was more than we actually spent, but it was useful to make the estimation, since we could go to the store to buy groceries without knowing exactly how much we would spend. Our estimate was reliable.

Estimates are often higher than the actual, eventual numbers, as they save us time and social embarrassment. After all, we do not want to go to the store and not have enough money to pay for the items we have placed on the checkout counter. It would embarrass us to have to take some of the groceries back to the shelf and make others in line wait longer. Estimation is a useful and powerful tool, because it allows us to act when we have only a limited set of information, rather than waiting for exact information before proceeding.

Making good estimates is one of the most important goals of early education. Young children must decide if an answer is a reasonable one, and if it is, to act upon it.

A word related to estimation is **prediction**. What's the difference? Prediction looks at a future event or problem and tries to answer it based on current observations. Estimates, on the other hand, attempt to provide an answer to a problem that exists right now.

Activities That Teach Computation

Adding Beads

Materials

PVC plumbing elbow with a drain
and screw-on drain cap
small plastic stringing beads of
various colors
clear plastic cup

Count on This

Children love adult tools! Look
around the house to see what you
can use for teaching math (an old
tape measure, carpenter's rule, nuts,
bolts, washers, and buttons).

In Addition

Hardware stores will be glad to order
you a plumbing elbow with screw
cap drain if they don't have one in
stock.

Math Objectives That Meet Standards

Children will:
1. Add and subtract numbers 1–10 using concrete objects.
2. Combine sets of objects to create a new set.

How to Do It

- Demonstrate this activity in Group Time and then move it to the Math or Games and Puzzles Center.
- At Group Time, show the children the PVC plumbing elbow.
- Take off the drain cap.
- Hold a clear plastic cup under the drain.
- Ask one child to stand on one side, holding three red beads, and another child to stand on the other side, holding two green beads.
- Tell the children to drop their beads into each side of the plumbing elbow at the same time. (See illustration.)
- The beads slide out of the drain as a combined set of green and red beads.
- Remove the beads from the plastic cup and count them.

Take It Up a Level

Glue the beads to a 3" x 6" heavy construction paper card. Write an addition sentence (for example: 3 + 2 = _____), leaving the answer blank. Ask the children to write the answer. After the children understand how the activity works, ask them to make their own addition cards.

Button Spill

Materials

gift bag
small brown paper lunch bag
marker
10 buttons (with distinct differences
between the front and back)
spray paint, if needed (adults only)
lunch tray
scissors
glue

Count on This

Group similar objects by number
when you talk about them. For
example, "Let's see, we have three
chairs near the bookcase and two
more next to the desk. We need them
together for all of us to sit down.
How many will we have? Is that
enough for all of us to have a seat?"
Group books, backpacks, shoes,
blocks, and children. This helps
develop the children's understanding
of math language.

Math Objectives That Meet Standards

Children will:
1. Recognize numerals.
2. Combine sets of objects to create a new set.
3. Add whole numbers up to 10 using concrete objects.

How to Do It

- Introduce this activity during Group Time, and then move it to the Math or Games and Puzzles Center. Ask a child to help you demonstrate this activity the first time.
- Put 10 buttons in the small brown paper lunch bag and write "Spill Bag" on the front. If the buttons do not have distinct differences between their fronts and backs, paint one side a certain color and the other side another color to distinguish the front and back.
- Put the lunch bag with the buttons and a lunch tray inside a large gift bag and set it out for the children.
- Show the children how to pull the tray and lunch bag from the gift bag and dump the buttons out of the lunch bag and onto the tray.
- Ask the children to count how many buttons have their fronts (or one color) showing and how many have their backs (or another color) showing.
- After the children say the correct numbers, ask them to count the total of the buttons aloud. Then help them make a number sentence using the buttons.

Take It Up a Level

Ask the children who can to write their own number sentence from the spilled button.

In Addition

For math activities, use buttons with cartoon figures painted on them. Children add cartoon character buttons quickly and more accurately than they count ordinary buttons. You can find specialty buttons at local fabric shops.

Adding Domino Dots

Materials

(per group)
seven or eight dominoes
large tray
basket
Post-it notes

Math Objectives That Meet Standards

Children will:
1. Add and subtract whole numbers 1–10 using concrete objects.
2. Combine and separate sets of objects to create a new set.

How to Do It

- Use dominoes as a quick way to get children excited about adding and subtracting.
- Put the dominoes in a small basket on the tray.
- Initially, demonstrate this activity to all the children together, and then let them continue it in groups of three or four in the Math Center.

- During this activity, walk around the groups, facilitating group decisions, and checking the accuracy of the children's answers.
- The children place all the dominoes face up. One at a time, ask them to select a domino, and ask each child to count aloud the dots on one side of the domino, then the dots on the other side.
- After the child counts the dots, ask the other children to add them together and help them write their answers on Post-it notes. The children stick the Post-it notes on the table next to the domino.
- Once the children are proficient at adding the numbers on the dominoes, challenge them to subtract the smaller number from the larger number. Rotate the domino so the largest number of dots is on the left and the small number of dots is on the right. Help the children subtract the number on the right from the number on the left, then write their answers on Post-it notes.
- Let the children collectively figure out the answer. For example, if the children decide that the answer is six, the group selects one child to write the answer on the Post-it and place it next to the domino. When the group is finished, check their answers, then let the children remove the Post-it notes and put the dominoes away.

Take It Up a Level

Have the children write the addition and subtraction operation in a number sentence (for example: *3 + 4 = 7*, or *4 − 3 = 1*).

Adding a Die-Inside-a-Die

Materials

clear plastic gift box (4" x 4" x 2")
die
permanent marker
clear packing tape

In Addition

Paper clips are often available in hard plastic boxes at office supply stores. Soft plastic boxes are available from many catalog companies, sometimes with erasers shaped like apples or zoo and farm animals. Both the boxes and the contents are useful for this activity, and generally good to have in your classroom.

Math Objectives That Meet Standards

Children will:
1. Add and subtract whole numbers 1–10 using concrete objects.
2. Combine and separate sets of objects to create a new set.

How to Do It

- Use a permanent marker to make dots on the inside of the clear plastic gift box and the lid so the box resembles a die. (See illustration.)
- Put an actual die inside the box, attach the lid, and tape it closed with clear plastic tape.
- Invite the children to roll the die-inside-a-die.
- When the gift box die settles, have the children add together the numbers on the top of box and the top of the die inside the box.

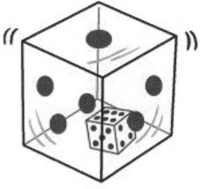

Take It Up a Level

When children are proficient at addition, challenge them to subtract the smaller number from the larger number.

12 Ways to Get to 11

Materials

12 Ways to Get to 11 by Eve Merriam
18" x 24" sheet of chart paper
black marker

Math Objectives That Meet Standards

Children will:
1. Add and subtract whole numbers 1–10, using concrete objects.
2. Recall basic addition and subtraction facts.
3. Learn sums to 10.

How to Do It

- Eve Merriam's *12 Ways to Get to 11* is a unique and delightful book about counting.
- Read the book to all the children, or in a small group setting, discussing each page with the children.
- The first page of the book combines nine and two to get 11, and each page gets progressively harder. The last page, for instance, combines *5 + 3 + 2 + 1 = 11*.
- As the children find the different number sets and combine them to get to 11, write on the number sentences on the chart paper in black marker.
- Because each book page stands on its own, you can go through as many pages as you want—do it a page a day, if you like.
- When you finish the book and the chart, place them in the Math Center for the children to look at and review.

Take It Up a Level

Challenge the children to combine number sets to make a larger number, such as 15.

Finger Ring Addition

Materials

50–60 plastic, pull-out caps from milk and juice cartons (they cover carton-lid openings and have a ring attached) (see illustration below)
permanent marker
basket

Math Objectives That Meet Standards

Children will:
1. Add and subtract whole numbers up to 10 using concrete objects.
2. Recall basic addition and subtractions facts, adding sums to 10.

How to Do It

- Use the permanent marker to write numerals 1–10 on the caps, creating a few copies of each number. Write a few addition, subtraction, and equal signs on some of the caps.
- The attached rings make great rings for small fingers.
- Encourage the children to put number rings on their fingers and add the numbers.
- The children can either count their fingers from 1–5, or write number sentences with the number rings (for example, *1 + 2 = 3*).

Take It Up a Level

Have the children use the pull-out caps to create and solve number sentences on their fingers.

Lunch Bag Number Book

Materials

brown paper lunch bag
markers
one sheet of white copy paper
stapler
scissors

Count on This

Most people, both children and adults, are more likely to follow instructions if they are in or on a bag rather than on a sheet of white paper. Curiosity? Perhaps.

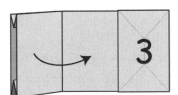

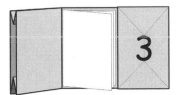

Staple edge

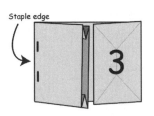

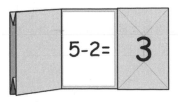

Math Objectives That Meet Standards

Children will:
1. Subtract and add whole numbers 1–10 using concrete objects.
2. Recall basic addition and subtraction facts, adding sums to 10.

How to Do It

- Put this activity in the Library Center. Even if children avoid the Math Center, math can sneak up on them when they do a math activity in the Library Center!
- Follow the instructions below to make a Lunch Bag Number Book (see illustration).
  1. Place the lunch bag horizontally, with the open end of the bag to your left, and the bottom flap facing up on the right side.
  2. Fold the open top half of the bag over to the right, so the open end of the bag is slightly under the bottom flap.
  3. Cut one sheet of white paper into four equal sections.
  4. Unfold the open end of the bag.
  5. Place the sheets of paper under the bag flap, positioning the left edge of each sheet along the crease made from folding the open end of the bag over.
  6. Fold the open side of the bag to the right, over the sheets of paper, positioning the top of the bag edge under the flap.
  7. Staple along the folded left edge of the bag, attaching the sheets of paper simultaneously.
  8. Write a number on the flap at the right end of the bag.
  9. On the left end of the bag, and on each of the sheets of paper, write different subtraction number sentences for which number on the right is the answer. (For example, if the number on the right end is 3, you might have number sentences such as $6-3 =$, $5-2 =$, and so on.)
- Select the numeral you want to use and write it on the bottom of the bag flap.
- Write a sample subtraction sentence on the side of the bag (see suggestions above) and then have the children fill in the remaining pages with other number sentences that equal that number.
- Give the children sheets of white paper and encourage them to write subtraction sentences for which the answers are the number on the bag flap (try this with addition sentences as well).

Take It Up a Level

- Help children who are developmentally ready make their own lunch bag number books.
- After the children have mastered addition sentences, encourage them to try subtraction sentences.

Addition on Fold-Out Flaps

Materials

8½" x 11" sheets of copy paper
black marker
overhead marker
basket

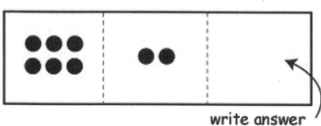

write answer

Math Objectives That Meet Standards

Children will:
1. Add and subtract whole numbers 1–10 using concrete objects.
2. Write numerals 1–10.
3. Understand that numbers represent the same quantity from object to object.
4. Recall basic addition and subtraction facts.
5. Add sums to 10.

How to Do It

○ Cut several 8½" x 11" sheets of paper into four equal 2¾" x 8½" lengths.

○ Fold each quarter-sheet into equal thirds.

○ On the first and second panels of each quarter sheet, draw die dots for the sums you want the children to add. For instance, make five dots on the left third of the sheet, and two dots on the middle third of the sheet. Leave the right third of the sheet blank.

○ Laminate and re-fold all of the strips.

　○ Challenge the children to count the dot combinations and write their answers in either dots or actual numbers on the right third of the sheets using an overhead marker. (See illustration.)

　○ Encourage the children to check each other's work. You can also make the activity self-checking by writing the answer in dots and number on the back the strip, so the children can turn over the sheet to check it themselves.

○ Put the strips and the overhead marker in the basket and put it in the Math Center.

Take It Up a Level

○ Show the children how to write a number sentence using math symbols (for example, *5 + 2 = 7*).

○ Show the children how to make their own fold-out flaps and challenge their friends with number sentences.

Block Building Cards

Materials

blocks
index cards
markers
large basket

Math Objectives That Meet Standards

Children will:
1. Count objects aloud.
2. Match the number of objects to a number that is the sum of the objects.
3. Recognize numbers.

How to Do It

○ This is a Block Center building activity.

○ Make a variety of building cards with one or several outlines of two different block shapes, and the number of them written beside the group of outlines (for example, three triangles and three column blocks).

○ Challenge the children to build with three triangle blocks and two rectangle blocks, or whatever combination of blocks comes up on their cards. Note: The silhouettes on the cards should match exactly the shapes of the blocks the children use to build with, because many children need to see the silhouettes to know which blocks to match them to. (See illustrations on appendix page 162 and 168.)

○ Place the building cards face down in the large basket.

○ Encourage children to choose a card, count aloud the numbers on the card, pick up that many of the types of blocks indicated on the card, and build a structure with them.

Library Pocket Math

Materials

three library pockets (use library pockets with colorful designs)
colored craft sticks
large gift bag (approximately 14½" x 9")
soft- and hook-side Velcro (with peel-and-stick backing)
scissors
4" x 6" colored index cards
glue

Math Objectives That Meet Standards

Children will:
1. Add and subtract whole numbers 1–10 using concrete objects.
2. Recall basic addition and subtraction facts.
3. Add sums to 10.

How to Do It

○ Glue three library pockets next to each other, about 1¼" apart, on the side of a large gift bag.

○ Cut several index cards into quarters, so there are four 2" x 3" rectangles made from each index card, and write the numerals 1–10 on two or three sets of the cutout rectangles.

○ Cut three 1" x 2" rectangles from an index card, and write a plus sign (+) on one, a minus sign (−) on another, and an equal sign (=) sign on the third.

○ Attach hook-side Velcro to the backs of all the number and sign cards, and soft-side Velcro on each of the library pockets, as well as in the two areas between the library pockets.

○ Put all the cards and several craft sticks in the gift bag, so the bag and the contents become the "Addition and Subtraction Center."

- Invite a child to select a number to put on each of the first two pockets and an addition or subtraction sign between those pockets, then place an equal sign after the second pocket (so the line reads, for example, *3 + 2 =*).
- After making the number sentence, have the child put the same number of craft sticks in each pocket as the numbers on the pockets (three sticks in the number 3 pocket and two sticks in the number 2 pocket, for example), then move all the sticks to the last pocket and count them to get the total.
- Once the child has the number total, 5, for example, ask him to find the index card with that numeral on it and put it on the last pocket.

Number Sentence Bracelet

Materials

buttons, large ones and small ones
lightweight, elastic thread
fine-point permanent marker

Count on This

- Many children love to string the buttons in order from 1–5. Make bracelets and let them walk around the room reading their number sentences to other children. They will love doing it!
- The Art Center is often the favorite center of struggling learners. Children enjoy going there because it is less academic and less threatening than some of the other centers. You can use the Art Center to "sneak" in some math activities.

Math Objectives That Meet Standards

Children will:
1. Add and subtract whole numbers up to 10 using concrete objects.
2. Recall basic addition and subtraction facts, sums to 10.
3. Combine and separate sets of objects to create a new set.

How to Do It

- Set up this activity in the Art Center.
- Set out several buttons and lengths of thread for the children.
- Write the math symbols plus (+), minus (–), and equals (=) on a set of larger buttons, one symbol per button.
- Cut 6"–8" lengths of elastic thread to accommodate the number of children that will be doing this activity.
- Put the buttons and the thread in a basket.
- To do the activity, a child puts a certain number of buttons on the string, say four, followed by a plus (+) sign, then another number of buttons on the string, say two, followed by a button with an equal (=) sign, and then six buttons on the right, so the number sentence is self-correcting. (See illustration.)

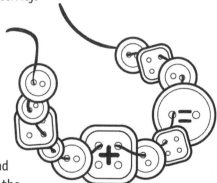

- Also, for children who are able, write the numbers 1–10 on several buttons, so a child can pull out a thread and slide the buttons with numbers on it to make a number sentence (such as *4 + 2 = 6*), then tie the bracelet together and wear it on his wrist.

Take It Up a Level

If the children are ready developmentally, have them string additional number sentences, such as *3 + 1 = 4 + 1 = 5 – 4 = 1 + 2 = 3*. Put them on their wrists and let the other children read the sentences.

Adding Using Playing Cards

Materials

math stand (see page 164)

deck of playing cards with the aces, kings, queens, jacks, and jokers removed

plus (+) and minus (–) signs cut from a 3" x 5" index card

8½" x 11" cardstock

Math Objectives That Meet Standards

Children will:

1. Add and subtract whole numbers up to 10 using concrete objects.
2. Recall basic addition and subtractions facts, sums to 10.

How to Do It

- The children do this activity in pairs in the Math Center using playing cards to form and solve number sentences, such as *5* (of diamonds) + *2* (of hearts) = *7* (of clubs).
- Trace three playing card outlines on cardstock, as shown in the illustration below.

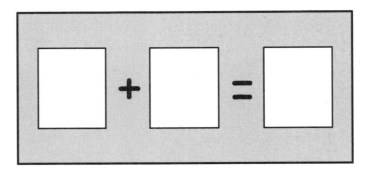

- Write an equal (=) sign between the second and third outlines.
- Laminate the cardstock, making the pattern board.
- Cut the 3" x 5" index card in half and write a plus (+) sign on each half. Laminate both pieces.
- Separate the cards into two piles, the "question" stack with numbers 2–5 in it, and the "answer" stack with numbers 4–10 in it. This way, the children won't have answers that exceed 10.
- One child in each pair sets out the piece of cardstock with the playing card outlines, pulls two playing cards from the "question" stack, and positions them on the first two outlines, then puts either the plus (+) or minus (–) sign between them.
- Challenge the second child to solve the number sentence by counting the number of suit symbols (hearts, spades, diamonds, clubs) on each card, adding or subtracting them to get a final number, then counting the suit symbols on the cards in the "answer" stack until he finds one with the matching number of suit symbols on it. The child then places it on the third blank on the pattern board.
- Encourage the children to take turns forming and solving the number sentences on the pattern board.

Take It Up a Level

When the children are ready, challenge them to solve subtraction number sentences.

License Plate Math

Math Objectives That Meet Standards

Children will:
1. Add and subtract whole numbers 1–10 using concrete objects.
2. Recall basic addition and subtraction facts, sums to 10.

Materials

license plate(s)
peeled crayons
copy paper

Count on This

Like almost everything young children do, guessing improves with age—it becomes estimating.

How to Do It

- Do this activity in the Art Center—it is a "backdoor" entry into the subject of math and it often interests children who typically avoid math.
  - Before the children do a rubbing of the license plate, suggest that they count the same number of objects as the numbers on the license plate. For example:
  - If the license plate reads CDR12, the children should count one and two of a certain object, such as crayons, before they make their rubbings.
  - The children then draw a dot with a crayons, so they see the final added number as three dots, corresponding to the three crayons they added based on the numbers 1 and 2 from the license plate.
- Show the children how to make rubbings over license plate letters and numbers.
- To make a rubbing, show the children how to place white paper over the license plate and use the side of a crayon to rub over the letters and numbers. As the children rub, the numbers and letters appear on the paper.
- Remove the plate. Tell the children to ignore the letters on the rubbing, and encourage them to add or subtract any of the numbers on the rubbing (see illustrations below).

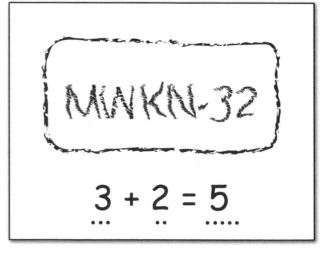

"Five Round Pumpkins"

Materials

Children who want to sing!

Math Objectives That Meet Standards

Children will:
1. Add and subtract whole numbers (1–5, 5–1).
2. Recall basic addition and subtraction facts (1–5, 5–1).

How to Do It

○ During Group Time or a small group setting, teach the children "Five Round Pumpkins."

○ After the children know the song, encourage them to make number sentences for each verse. (For more activity ideas with this song, see *Everyday Discoveries: Amazingly Easy Science and Math Activities with Stuff You Already Have* or *Jingle in My Pocket Book*, both by Sharon MacDonald.)

Five Round Pumpkins (Tune: "Five Little Honey Buns")
(From the *Jingle in My Pocket* CD, by Sharon MacDonald)

Five round pumpkins in a roadside store,
One became a jack-o-lantern, then there were four.

Four round pumpkins as orange as can be,
One became a pumpkin pie, then there were three.

Three round pumpkins with nothing fun to do,
One was cooked as pumpkin bread, then there were two.

Two round pumpkins sitting in the sun,
One was cooked as pancakes, then there was one.

One round pumpkin, one job was left undone,
He was kept to make new seeds, then there were none.

One round pumpkin, one job was left undone,
He was kept to make new seeds, then there were none.

Activities That Teach Estimation

Model Estimation Station

Materials

two small jars or plastic containers
    to hold pebbles

10 pebbles

marker

laminated "If ___, then ____?"
    board made from heavy cardstock

Sticky Tack

tray

small basket

pieces of paper cut to fit the bottom
    of the basket

pencils

estimation answer box (shoebox
    with a slit cut through its top)

1–20 number line

Math Objectives That Meet Standards

Children will:

1. Use estimation to predict computations to determine the reasonableness of answers.
2. Use estimation to predict computations in real-life situations.
3. Use numbers to make realistic predictions and estimates.

How to Do It

○ Create an estimation station on which the children can do this activity (see illustration below).

1. Place a sheet of construction paper on the bottom of a tray.
2. Put the basket of paper, the estimation answer box, and several pencils on the tray.
3. In the left bottom corner of the paper on the tray write "If" and on the right bottom corner, write "Then."
4. Above each word, place a jar and circle the outline with a marker.

○ Put a jar with three pebbles in it on the left circle, above the word "If." Attach it to the paper with Sticky Tack so the children cannot lift it.

○ Write, "If this jar has three pebbles" on a piece of paper, and attach it to the three-pebble jar.

- Place a jar with seven pebbles in it above the "Then," and write, "Then how many pebbles are in this jar?" on another piece of paper, and attach it to the seven-pebble jar.
- Invite the children to inspect the two jars, letting them pick up the jar with seven pebbles.
- After looking at the jars, give each child a sheet of paper so they can write an estimate of how many pebbles are in the second jar, and then put their written estimations in the answer box.
- At the end of the week, put the number line on the tray, have the children remove the pebbles from the container and, starting at 1, place them next to each number on the number line.
- When they learn how many pebbles were in the container, take out the estimates from the answer box and invite the children to check them for accuracy.

Estimation Station Ideas

Materials

materials to estimate, such as seeds, paper clips, buttons, crayons, dog biscuits, ice cubes, raindrops, marbles, rocks, people, feathers, leaves, apples, cotton balls, bones, flowers

box, basket, jar, tub, cup, pocket, or thimble to hold materials

scales to weigh materials

Count on This

Ask the children questions that require more than "yes" or "no" answers. For example, "What would happen if____?" "How can you find out about that?" It energizes children when they help to find solutions.

Math Objectives That Meet Standards

Children will:

1. Use estimation to predict quantities in real-life situations.
2. Identify situations involving whole numbers in which estimation is useful.
3. Use estimation to predict the reasonableness of computed answers.

How to Do It

- In the Estimation Station, set up different problems using boxes, baskets, jars, tubs, cups, pockets, or thimbles.
- Pose questions to the children, such as those listed below.
  - If this jar has five, then how many does this jar have? (Quantity)
  - How many marbles are in the jar? (Volume)
  - How much does the rock weigh? (Weight)
  - How many beads will it take to fill a box, basket, jar, tub, cup, pocket, or thimble? (Area)
  - How many crayons will it take to measure the length of a table, a building, door, or a child? (Length)
  - How many crayons will the whole class will use this year? (Time)
- Change your estimation activities weekly. Use new materials or objects with new questions. Consider estimating the following:
  - the number of ways to make a certain amount,
  - the time it takes to perform a certain activity,
  - the temperature of objects at different times,
  - the lengths of objects,
  - how many scoops of different objects are possible,
  - the age of items in years and days,
  - the number of steps it takes to get to a certain place or to complete an activity,
  - the pressure needed to move an object, and
  - objects' weights, heights, circumference, and values.

Estimation Station

Materials

designated estimation station (keep up all year—see suggestion on page 48, "a Model Estimation Station")

objects and materials, such as coins, rocks, leaves, paper clips, pieces of chalk, crayons, plastic ants, bolts, pompoms, or ice cubes

two same-size unbreakable jars

In Addition

Over time, alter the estimation activities so the children's guessing evolves from *how many* to more specific questions, such as *how long, how hot, how much, how often, how far, how much, how tall,* and so on.

Math Objectives That Meet Standards

Children will:

1. Use estimation to predict computations in real-life situations.
2. Identify situations involving whole numbers in which estimation is useful.
3. Use estimation to predict computations to determine the reasonableness of answers.

How to Do It

- Decide what objects and materials the children will use to make their estimations. Start with the simple and familiar, and move to more complex objects and materials.
- Use the "If _____, then _____" board (see "Model Estimation Station" on page 48). Using this board helps children become better estimators and lays the foundation for the scientific process of inquiry (scientific method) that the children will encounter later in their education.
- The "If _____, then _____" board changes depending on what the children are using for their estimations. For example, the board will look different when estimating the number of pompoms in a jar, or using boxes to estimate weight. The first jar (or box) is the "control" jar. The second jar is the "estimate" jar. The absolute number in either jar does not matter. The relative size is what matters, depending on the objects or materials used. The purpose of the activity is for the children to make better estimates using visual clues.
- Every week, put an estimation activity in the estimation station. Use an estimation box for the children to put their written estimates in during the week. At Group Time on Friday, review the children's estimates with them to see how well they are doing with developing and improving their estimating skills. The purpose of the activity is for children to look at objects in the jars (pick up visual clues in the environment), guess, and record their guesses.

Throughout-the-Day Estimates

Materials

Just children!

Math Objectives That Meet Standards

Children will:

1. Use estimations in real-life situations.
2. Identify situations involving whole numbers in which estimation is useful.
3. Use estimation to determine the reasonableness of answers.

How to Do It

- This is an especially good transition activity.
- The simplicity of this activity masks its effectiveness. Often, the most important learning happens informally, not during the process of teaching a lesson.

- Throughout the day, as children use different objects, such as markers, jump ropes, or blocks, ask them questions, such as:
  - How many do you think there are?
  - How long do you think it will take?
  - How much does that weigh?
  - How many steps to the cafeteria?

Pompom Grab

Materials

2½ gallon re-sealable plastic bag filled with pompoms

Count on This

What is important about learning to use estimation as a tool is to emphasize the importance of getting close to the answer, not getting the right answer.

Math Objectives That Meet Standards

Children will:
1. Identify situations involving whole numbers in which estimation is useful.
2. Name the number of objects there are in a group of three to five without counting.

How to Do It

- Do this activity any time you have a few extra minutes.
- Keep a plastic bag of pompoms handy and whenever there is time to fill, ask a child to reach into the bag and grab five pompoms.
- When a child thinks he has five, ask him to check the accuracy of his grab by counting the pompoms.
- At first, the children will grab big handfuls but as they become better estimators, they will start grabbing smaller amounts that are more accurate.

Estimation Jar or Box

Materials

plastic jar or box the children can carry home and bring back later
paper and pen or marker

In Addition

Use estimation words, such as *like, almost, near, approximately, in between, around, more than,* and *less than,* when you talk with the children.

Math Objectives That Meet Standards

Children will:
1. Use estimation to predict the reasonableness of computed answers.
2. Use estimation to predict computations in real-life situations.
3. Use numbers to make realistic predictions and estimates.
4. Count aloud from 1–10.

How to Do It

- Each Friday, send a child home with an empty jar or box, asking the child to put something in it that the class can use for estimating during the following week.
- Set up some criteria for what sort of items the children should bring to class in the container. For example, food will spoil and sharp things stick or cut, so it is best not to include them. Examples of acceptable items include pebbles, coins, leaves, twigs, paper clips, plastic animals, or pencils. With the children, make a list of acceptable objects, and hang the list near the estimation station.

- Talk about appropriate quantities for the children to bring to class. For example, why bring 100 items when most of the children can count only to 10 or 20?
- Explain to the children that they should only bring in as many items as the children are able to count (from 10–20 would be a reasonable amount).
- When a child brings the container to school, bring it to the "Model Estimation Station" (see page 48). Put some of the objects into the "If" jar, and two or three times that many in the "Then" jar, and challenge the children to estimate how many are in the "Then" jar.

Measurement, Seriation, Time, and Money

CHAPTER 4

What Is ...?

Measurement is finding the amount of something and giving it a number in units. This makes it possible to compare the number unit of one thing to the number units of others. Simply stated, measurement answers questions, such as, "Is it more, less, or the same?" Measurements are typically taken in standard units like inches, but it is also possible to take measurements in nonstandard units, like the length of a shoe.

What Is ...?

Seriation encompasses all aspects of measuring. Seriation means the arrangement of objects in a series by some prescribed criteria, such as size, shape, color, weight, length, or texture. To seriate by size, for example, is to put objects in order from smallest to largest or largest to smallest. To seriate by distance, a more abstract measurement, ask, "Which house is farthest away?" "Which is the next farthest away?" "Which is closest?" To seriate by volume, for example, to compare the amount of liquid in several jars, ask, "Which jar is fullest?" "Which jar is next?" "And the next?"

Showing young children how to seriate helps them to notice slight differences among objects, and new parts of the brain become more finely tuned and developed. Seriation incorporates both standard measurements, such as weighing pumpkins on a scale, and nonstandard measurements, such as putting pumpkins in order by size. Moving between nonstandard and standard measurement is excellent work for young children's developing brains.

What Is ...?

Time is how we pay for our lives. We count time in standard units that measure one moment to another. Most of us search for interesting ways to structure our time. Young children try to structure their time with new experiences.

A Few Words About Timers

A few activities in this chapter use timers, so it is important to know something about them. Standard kitchen ("tick, tick, tick") timers and the ones shaped like apples, oranges, eggs, or cows are not good timers to use in the early childhood classroom. They are for adults.

Things to Seriate

Below is a partial list of things to seriate. Use a standard measuring tool, such as a tape measure, to seriate these materials and record the data. There are lots of others, so think outside the pumpkin!

Length
Twigs
Crayons
Leaves
Lines drawn to different lengths
Shoes
Feathers

Size
Balls
Pizza-box lids
Pompoms
Toy cars and trucks
Boxes

Weight
Rocks
Baby dolls
Children
Apples, oranges, bananas, grapes, melons, and peaches
Beanbags

Circumference
Twigs
Pencils, crayons, and markers
Cylinder blocks (from the Block Center)
Cans
Jars

Height
Children
Tables, bookcases, and chairs
Steps of a ladder
Plants

Rough and Smooth
Sandpaper
Fabric

You need a really snazzy timer that captures the children's interest and curiosity. You are getting close to the right kind of timer if yours looks like an hourglass (the larger the better). There are 1-, 3-, and 5-minute timers.

I especially like two-minute timers to use to time the activities on the One Minute List on page 64. My favorite timers, though, come in brilliant colors with compartmented designs. They are called acrylic, water-wheel, and liquid timers. They are manufactured in plastic casings with interesting stuff inside, like beads, wheels, and glitter. Young children think they are the greatest invention since swings.

The Vocabulary of Time

Time has a vocabulary all its own. We all have our own personal experience of it. Time can be about a sequence ("What happens next?"), or it can be about duration ("How long is this going to take?").

There are several kinds of time, too. Most of us never think of time in different ways until someone points out the differences: we live in the moment without paying too much attention to the kind of a moment it is. There is your personal experience of time, indicated by a sentence beginning, for instance, "Yesterday, I..." There are the acts you perform to fill time: "I got up, got dressed, ate breakfast, and went to work." There is the clock-and-calendar time of our everyday lives, cultural time.

The clock and calendar drive modern society. Young children have a hard time learning cultural time, however, until they are ready to defer many of their immediate needs.

Language is a big part of time measurement. Young children frequently hear time-related language when they begin preschool. They might hear, "How old are you?" "...in five minutes." "Did you have a good time?" "We will do that tomorrow." "Please do it right now!" Most children, however, do not yet understand what the words mean, or that time is a standard measurement, measured in the same way from one place to another.

Children are bound by their experiences of time. If you ask a child, for example, how long one minute is, you will get different responses depending on the situation. There are long minutes and short ones. If the children are a minute away from having lunch, for example, it will be a long minute. If playtime will be over in one minute, on the other hand, it will be a short minute. (That's often how it is for adults, too—doing something pleasurable seems to end quickly and waiting for an anticipated event seems to take a long time.)

About Timers

- Colorful, apparently intricate timers get lots of attention. The other kinds don't.
- A wide variety of timers are available from many catalogs and Web sites, including www.RainbowSymphonyStore.com and www.OfficePlayground.com.

It's About Time!

Words about time happen frequently. Here are just a few. Be sure to use them frequently: *soon, tomorrow, yesterday, a long time ago, late, early, once upon a time, new, old, now, when, sometimes, then, before, while, never, next always, fast, slow, first, second, morning, noon, night, evening, day, afternoon.*

To help the children develop a sense of time passing, ask them to jump for a minute and count their jumps as they go. Set a timer. After about 15 seconds, one of the children will likely stop to ask whether the timer is broken, because the experience of time when jumping in place, counting each jump, makes a minute feel very long.

What Is ...?

Money is how we pay for the things we want. It is a measurement of value. We begin by learning to count money, and then we try to figure out what to buy with it. It is a vastly complicated subject, one difficult even for adults. It is understandable that young children can have difficulty learning about money.

Developmental Stages of Measurement

This chapter focuses on measuring length, temperature, weight, volume, time, and money. Young children develop predictably through physical and mental stages of everything they do, even how they measure things. Four overlapping levels encompass the children's understanding of measurement:

Level 1: Children imitate adult behavior. They watch adults measure things and mimic the action. They use similar tools and movements but they really do not understand that they are measuring a quantity of something and giving it a number. Their awareness of the physical space around them becomes apparent in their speech. For example, children indicate awareness of:

- temperature, by saying, "It's too hot,"
- height, by saying, "That's up too high,"
- weight, by saying, "This is too heavy," or
- volume, by saying, "It all spilled out."

Level 2: Children start to compare. A child may know, for instance, that Joe's cookie is bigger than her cookie. The measurement units are: *bigger, smaller, heavier, lighter, longer, shorter, hotter,* and *colder.*

Level 3: Children start using nonstandard units of measurement. They measure using blocks, rocks, or shoes. They don't need for others to get the same answers they got, since it is not important to them that results match up. They just need to know an object's length. Therefore, "10 shoes long" works for them.

Level 4: Children learn to value and start to apply standard units of measurement. Typically, this happens because the children want to get the same results as their friends or because they predict certain outcomes and want them to be correct. When making cookies, for instance, the children see that it is important to measure the correct amount of each ingredient. Applying standard units of measurement will ensure their cookies come out right.

Activities That Teach Measurement

Tape Measure

Materials

tape measures (one per child)

Count on This

Modeling is the best teaching tool. It reduces anxiety because children can see what they are supposed to do before they have to do it. For example, in the Block Center in my classroom, I had a basket with several tape measures. I began to measure different things in the classroom and comment on the measurements. The children began to measure different items. By the end of the year, we had measured everything in the room and most things on the playground. We had made charts and graphs of what we had measured, and we had talked about other measuring tools, like the yardstick and the ruler. The children counted to 36, they knew how to measure using inches, feet, and yards. Modeling works. It is reinforced by getting out of the way to let learning happen.

Math Objectives That Meet Standards

Children will:
1. Understand and use standard measurement.
2. Use measurement vocabulary when comparing lengths.

How to Do It

- Get ready! When children master the skills in this activity, they will want to measure everything in the classroom.
- Set out a basket of tape measures. Be sure there is one for every child, because they will all want to be able to use a tape measure at the same time.
- Model how to use the tape measure. Be casual! The value is in making the comparisons, not getting the accurate results. Measure the children's arms, the diameter of their heads, the distance between chairs, and the height of tables. When outside, measure the length of the jump rope, the height of plants, and the distance from the slide to the water table, among other things. The children will ask what you are up to. They will want to do it too.
- When the children ask, talk about what you are measuring and make comparisons. For example, "Oh, Jason's wrist is 3" around and Carrie's is 2" around. I wonder whose wrist is bigger?" or "This shelf is 6" long and this one is 12" (or 1'). Which one is longer?"
- Invite the children to pick a tape measure and measure objects, and compare their results among themselves. The children will want to measure everything, and you can stand back and watch. In fact, this activity works best when you get out of the way and let things happen.
- As the days continue and the children measure more objects in the room, begin making charts and graphs indicating the length of the items measured.
- Talk with the children about other measuring tools, like the yardstick and the ruler.
- This activity will help the children learn the values of and how to distinguish among inches, feet, and yards.

In Addition

Use crayons for nonstandard measurement (for example, "How many crayons long is your shoe?") Use other objects for nonstandard measurement, like blocks, hands, feet, paper clip links, Unifix Cubes, 1" cubes, and other commercially available products.

Daily Temperature

Materials

red, orange, yellow, green, blue, and
  purple crayons
45"–46" length of white ribbon
clear packing tape
red permanent marker
outdoor thermometer (see illustration)
poster board
quart-size, storage bags with zipper
  closures
smaller thermometer
scissors

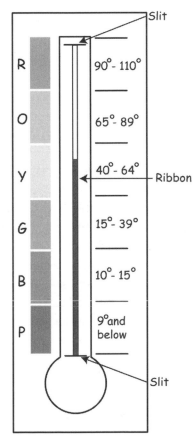

Count on This

Visuals create attention and interest,
and they add pleasure to children's
learning experience.

Math Objectives That Meet Standards

Children will:

1. Use and understand the benefit of standard measurement.
2. Understand measurement vocabulary of *hotter* and *colder*.
3. Compare temperatures.
4. Identify temperature-measuring instruments.
5. Count by 1s.

How to Do It

- Set up a thermometer outside in a place where it is visible from a window or door of the classroom.
- Set up the large, poster board thermometer, shown in the illustration, in front of the children when they meet for Group Time. To make the poster board thermometer, follow the instructions below:
  1. Draw and cut out a large thermometer (28" x 12") from a sheet of poster board, drawing the hash marks that indicate different degrees on the right side of the shape.
  2. Cut a slit in the bottom of the thermometer and one at the top of the thermometer. Come down 2" from the top and the bottom and make the slit 1" long from side to side.
  3. Cut approximately 45" of white ribbon. Use the red marker to color one-half of the white ribbon. Slip the ribbon in the top slit and the bottom slit. Tape it together with a 1" overlap. Make sure that when you pull up or down on the ribbon it moves easily.
  4. Color temperature intervals along the left side of the thermometer: 90°–110°, red; 65°–89°, orange; 40°–64°, yellow; 15°–39°, green; 10°–15° blue; and, 9° and below, purple. These temperature intervals are suggestions; adjust temperatures to fit the weather in your geographic area.
- Help the children make their own smaller versions of the thermometer. To do so, follow the instructions below:
  1. Make copies (one per child) of the small thermometer illustration (see appendix page 165), and follow the assembly instructions below.
  2. Color the thermometer shape with the appropriate descending color scheme similar to the poster board thermometer above.
  3. Put the cutout of the thermometer shape inside the quart baggie and close it, keeping the thermometer shape flush against the zip lining.
  4. Trim the excess baggie plastic and throw it away, then tape the baggie back together, so it holds the thermometer shape snugly.

As part of daily Group Time activities, choose a child to serve as the weather reporter for the day. Let the reporter for the day choose a partner to go along outside to confirm her measurements (one of the children will usually come back with the right answer). Encourage the children to read the thermometer, set their baggie thermometers to match by moving the zipper closure opposite the temperature, and then bring their findings back to the rest of the children.

○ Invite the weather reporter to move the ribbon on the poster board thermometer to match her temperature report.

○ After the weather reporter sets the poster board thermometer accordingly, invite the children to set their own thermometers to match it.

Track the Weather

Materials

days-in-the-school-year number line (a number line that begins with "Day 1" on the first day of school and ends with the last day of the school year)

3½" construction-paper squares in the colors red, orange, yellow, green, blue, and purple

Math Objectives That Meet Standards

Children will:

1. Use and understand the benefit of standard measurement.
2. Understand measurement vocabulary of *hotter* and *colder*.
3. Compare temperature.
4. Identify temperature-measuring instruments.
5. Count by ones.

How to Do It

○ Track the daily temperature on a days-in-the school-year number line.

○ Set up the number line at the children's height in the classroom.

○ Each day, when the weather reporter pulls the ribbon to the correct outside temperature (see "Daily Temperature" on the previous page), help her write the temperature on a colored piece of paper that corresponds to the color beside the day's temperature on the thermometer. For example, if the temperature is 75° outside (in the orange range on the poster board thermometer), you or the reporter would write "75" on an orange, 3½" square of paper. If the temperature is 25° (in the green range on the poster board thermometer), you or the reporter would write "25" on a green square.

In Addition

Teach the children the American Sign Language sign for "temperature" (see illustration). It is important for children to learn that people have many ways to talk to one other. One example is sign language. We use sign language to talk to people who cannot hear well.

American Sign Language sign for "temperature"

- After writing the daily temperature on the square, have the weather reporter attach it under the correct day in the days-in-the-school-year number line using Sticky Tack or clear plastic tape. For example, if it is the 45th day of the school year, and 25° outside, the reporter would attach a 3½" green "25" construction-paper square under the 45th day of the school year.

- Set out pictures or drawings that relate temperature to people's behavior and invite the children to attach the images below each day's temperature reading on the number line. For example, when it is 90° outside, have the child put up a picture of a person fanning herself at the beach. When it is 25°, have the child put up a picture of a person skiing.

Take It Up a Level

Ask the children to bring a calendar to school. Each day, after recording the temperature on the number line, invite the children to color the corresponding day's square in their calendars. They will keep track of the actual days of the week and months of the year, while also giving the children a visual sense of the changes in the weather as the year progresses.

Kitchen Scale

Materials

large kitchen scale
rocks, crayons, blocks, pencils, and buttons to weigh

Count on This

Consider using pompoms with small differences in their sizes to challenge the children. The more you use pompoms, the better off you'll be. They are soft, squishy, and fuzzy. You can toss them and they fall to the floor quietly. They don't cost much. Many catalog companies have a variety of pompoms in different colors and sizes.

Math Objectives That Meet Standards

Children will:
1. Weigh materials using standard measurement.
2. Understand the benefit of using standard measurement.
3. Compare weights.
4. Count by ones.

How to Do It

- Set up the activity in the Math or Science Center.
- Using the kitchen scale, weigh several of one type of object at a time, such as rocks, crayons, blocks, pencils, or buttons.
- Encourage the children to sort and organize them based on specific characteristics unique to each type of object. If you have buttons, for example, sort them by color.
- Ask the children to weigh the red buttons and the yellow buttons. Ask, "Which weighs more?"
- If you have buttons in other colors, ask the children to weigh them. For example, do the 10 purple buttons weigh more than the 10 green ones?
- Give the children a new challenge each day or at the beginning of each week.
- When they tire of the buttons, use rocks, sorted by different characteristics, to weigh and compare.

In Addition

Buy used kitchen scales at junk stores, flea markets, and garage sales. They usually work surprisingly well, and, if they are a little off, remember that in the early years, we are primarily interested in having the children make comparisons, using measurement, and becoming familiar with tools and numbers, not finding the "right" answers.

After the children are familiar with all the materials, put three of them out at a time so the children can do mixed comparisons. Encourage the children to talk about their comparisons. For example, ask, "Do three rocks weigh the same as six green buttons?"

Take It Up a Level

Make index cards available for the children to document their findings when they weigh and compare the different materials. Encourage them to use "If _____, then _____" statements, and ask the children questions such as "Is the result greater than (>) ___? Less than (<) ___? Or equal to (=) ___?" or, "What is the answer?" depending on their abilities.

Charting Children's Weights

Materials

6' tape measure
bathroom scale
chart paper with "How much do I weigh?" written across the top
markers

Count on This

Some children may be sensitive about their weight. Let the children decide if they want to weigh themselves. They may want to make up a number. That's OK. They may decide not to do the activity at all. That's OK, too.

Math Objectives That Meet Standards

Children will:
1. Recognize that a bathroom scale measures weight in pounds.
2. Understand the benefits of using standard measurement.
3. Use measurement vocabulary, such as *more, less*, and *the same as*.

How to Do It

- Select a spot in the classroom to weigh the children.
- Put the chart above the bathroom scale.
- Weigh the children, one at a time. Write each child's name on the chart. Let them read the bathroom scale and tell you how much they weigh (double check for accuracy), and write the weight next to each child's name.
- When you finish weighing all the children, remove the chart, and put it up in the classroom so the children can see it during Group Time.
- Talk about the different weights of the children in the classroom.

Measuring Children's Heights

Materials

adding machine tape
any two colors of paper
clear packing tape
tape measure
Sticky Tack
Adding machine tape measurements
of children

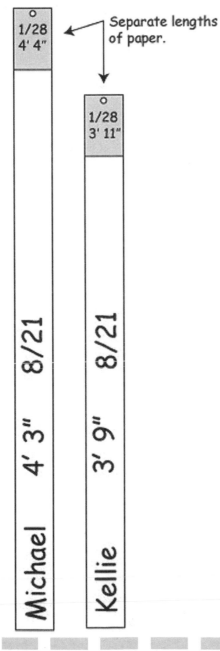

Separate lengths of paper.

Math Objectives That Meet Standards

Children will:
1. Measure and compare height using nonstandard measurement.
2. Use measurement vocabulary such as taller, shorter, longer, and so on.

How to Do It

- The first time you do this activity should be at the beginning of the school year.
- Measure one child at a time, asking each to stand with her heels and the back of her head against the wall.
- Roll out the adding machine tape, running it from her feet to her head.
- Measure the length of tape with the tape measure.
- Write the child's name, date, and height in feet and inches on the tape (use a tape measure to convert height to feet and inches).
- Hang the adding machine tape with Sticky Tack.
- When all the children have had their heights measured, put the children into small groups of three or four children and have them select who in their groups have the longest (tallest) lengths of tape.
- Come back together as a class and sort all the tapes by height.
- In January, repeat the activity. Instead of using another long piece of adding machine tape, attach a strip of colored paper to the top of the previous tape using clear packing tape.
- Record the date and height on a colored paper strip. The color change shows the number of inches the child has grown.
- You may have to reorder the tape from tallest to shortest because a child has had a large growth spurt.
- At the end of the year, do the activity the last time, adding a different colored paper strip to each earlier tape.
- The tape captures each child's physical growth throughout the entire school year. Children are always up for this activity, and look forward to making comparisons.

Measuring with Pompoms

Materials

pompoms in a large basket
items to measure
chart paper with "Pompom
   Measuring" written at the top
markers

In Addition

A great book to use with this
activity is *The Line Up Book* by
Marisabina Russo. In the book, a
child uses books, boots, and other
things to measure the distance from
her bedroom to the kitchen.

Math Objectives That Meet Standards

Children will:
1. Compare lengths.
2. Measure everyday objects using nonstandard measurement.
3. Use measurement vocabulary, such as *short, long, more than, less than*, and *the same as*.

How to Do It

- Select a different object to measure each time you do this activity.
- Write the activity name on the chart paper (select from the list below).

Pompom Measurement Activity List:
- distance to the door
- width of the doorway
- width of the table
- length of the bookcase
- length of the chalk tray
- width of the counter
- width across the sink
- length of a child lying on the floor
- length of an object on the table or the floor
- circumference of a round rug

- Put the chart paper up on the wall at the children's height, and place a basket of pompoms below.
- After the children make their measurements with pompoms, help them record their findings on the chart, and put their names next to their results.
- It is helpful to draw picture directions so those children who have difficulty reading the words can still do the activity.

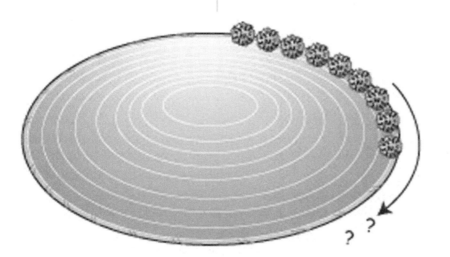

Activities That Teach Seriation

Seriate Paint Color Sample Cards

Materials

paint color sample cards
silhouette board (see illustration)
silhouette boards for four paint
    sample cards

Paint cards

In Addition

Teach volume! How many balls will go in that basket? How many socks will fill that boot? How many cups of water will fill that pail?

Math Objectives That Meet Standards

Children will:
1. Compare and sequence objects from light and dark and dark to light.

How to Do It

- Set up this activity in the Math Center.
- Paint color sample cards, available from home improvement stores, come with three to eight different color shades on each card. Use just one card (one color with different shades).

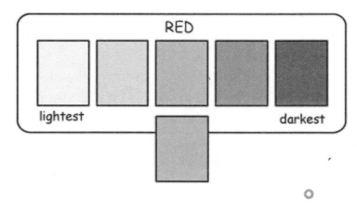

Laminate and cut apart the individual color shades. Use more shades, or fewer, depending on the age and skill level of the children. Even though the children in your class may be the same age, some may be able to seriate three colors while others may be able to seriate eight colors.

- Put the silhouette card (see illustration above) and the paint cards in a basket in the Math Center.
- Invite the children to place the cards on the silhouette board in order from darkest to lightest and lightest to darkest.

Count on This

Expand the activity, at the same skill level, by seriating by the characteristics of the materials below:

- sandpaper (by roughness)
- fabric (by texture)
- objects with other physical characteristics: softness, hardness, color shade, weight, height, temperature, and volume
- rocks, leaves, twigs, pencils, paper clips, and books

Pompom Seriation

Math Objectives That Meet Standards

Children will:

1. Compare and sequence objects.
2. Use measurement vocabulary.

Materials

pompoms of various sizes (five to 10, depending on the children's abilities)

tray

How to Do It

○ Demonstrate the activity during Group Time and then set it up in the Math Center.
○ Place the pompoms on a tray.
○ Invite the children to place the pompoms in order by size from largest to smallest or smallest to largest.
○ For younger children, consider putting out a piece of paper with circles on it that correspond to the size of each pompom, in descending size.

Activities That Teach About Time

The-In-One-Minute List

Math Objectives That Meet Standards

Children will:

1. Use language associated with time in everyday situations.
2. Begin to categorize activities in intervals of time.
3. Sequence events by duration of time.

Materials

construction paper or cardstock (cut in the shape of a clock, optional)

marker

How to Do It

○ This activity works best during Group Time.
○ Challenge the children to think of things they can do in about one minute.
○ As the children come up with ideas, ask them to perform the activities, and time them with a clock as they do them. Which ones actually take about one minute? Which take longer? Which take less time?
○ Draw those activities that take about a minute on the construction paper clock cutout, and write "One-Minute List" at the top of the page.
○ Some of the one-minute activities that children suggest include:
  ○ put on my socks,
  ○ button my shirt (blouse),
  ○ zip up my jacket,
  ○ eat a spoonful of peanut butter,
  ○ eat a banana,
  ○ write my name using all the letters,

○ peel the paper off a crayon, and
○ wait in line for water (sometimes!).

○ About one third of the activities suggested took about one minute. We put a minus sign (–) next to the ones that took less and a plus sign (+) next to the activities that took more than one minute.
○ Post the One-Minute List in the Math Center afterward for the children to add to and review.

Take It Up a Level

Post the chart in the Math Center with a marker so the children can write more one-minute activity ideas when they think of them.

Using a Timer to Time Events

Materials

timers

Math Objectives That Meet Standards

Children will:
1. Use language associated with time in everyday situations.
2. Begin to categorize time intervals.
3. Sequence events by duration.

How to Do It

○ Set out a timer. Challenge the children to predict the following, and think of other things to predict:
  ○ how long it takes to walk to the door, down the hall, to the gym, to the playground, or to the cafeteria;
  ○ how long it would take to put on a jacket and zip it, tie shoes, brush teeth, button a shirt, braid hair, or put on a smock;
  ○ how long a child can play with a toy, be in a center, have a turn, paint, mix the playdough, write a list, or clean the room; or
  ○ how long before the school day ends, the bus comes, the field trip or party starts, the pictures are taken, outside play begins, and when they can have snack or lunch.
○ Compare the children's time predictions to the timed results.

Timeline of Important School Events

Materials

sandwich-size baggies
4" x 6" (or 3" x 5") index cards
ribbon
days-in-the-school-year number line
    (from "Track the Weather" on
    page 58)

Count on This

Photograph the children doing different classroom activities. The photos will be a big draw because children love to see themselves in action.

Math Objectives That Meet Standards

Children will:
1. Identify tools used to measure intervals of time.
2. Sequence events by duration.
3. Name days of the week and months of the year.

How to Do It

- Throughout the school year, take photographs of significant events, such as a firefighter's visit to the class.
- Select a photograph of the event and glue it to an index card.
- Write the date on the bottom in large print.
- Put the index card with the photograph in a baggie.
- Use Sticky Tack to attach the baggie above the number line of the school day on which the event occurred.
- Use a length of ribbon to "connect" the baggie to the date on the number line.
- For example, If a firefighter comes to school on the 33rd school day of the year, take a photograph of his or her visit. Glue the photograph on the index card and write the date below it.
- Put the baggie above "33" on the number line. Use a length of ribbon to connect the bottom of the index card with the photo of the firefighter's visit (in the baggie) to the square of the 33rd day of school.

← 24   25 / 26   27   28   29   30 →

Number line with index card-backed photos and ribbon attached

- Other activities you might want to consider documenting with photographs, so you will have a wonderful record of the school year include the following:
    - a child's first lost tooth
    - birthdays
    - field trips
    - school visitor
    - pet day
    - parent night
    - special projects

Take It Up a Level

As events occur, make a timeline from photographs in baggies. Date each photograph and mark the event on the timeline. When you take the timeline down, make it into a class book.

Timeline of photographs folded like a fan into a book

Announcement Clock

Materials

cardboard clock, or cardboard, black
    poster board, scissors, marker,
    brad
clothespins
wall clock
marker

Count on This

Often, children's challenging behavior occurs because they do not know what is going to happen next. Think of ways to keep them "in the loop," letting them know when, where, and how things will happen.

Math Objectives That Meet Standards

Children will:
1. Tell time using an analog clock.
2. Sequence events by duration of time.

How to Do It

- Lower your classroom wall clock to about 2' above the children's heads, just beyond their reach.
- Use a purchased cardboard clock or follow these directions to make one:
    1. Cut out a cardboard circle about the same size as the wall clock, and write numbers around it, just as on a clock face.
    2. Cut out two hands of the clock from black poster board.
    3. Make a hole in the end of each hand and in the center of the clock.
    4. Attach the hands to the clock face with a brad.
- Place the cardboard clock under the classroom clock.
- On clothespins, write the names of different activities that will occur during the day.
- Fix the hands of the cardboard clock to the time of one of the events, and attach that activity's clothespin at that time. If you will be having a party at 2:00, for instance, write "Party" on the clothespin and clip it to the 2 on the cardboard clock face.
- When a child asks, "When's the party?" send her to the clocks to compare the two times and figure out the time remaining until the party.
- If a child does not understand the time differences, suggest that she ask a friend to explain it to her. She will be happier once she is "in the loop." If the friend cannot explain it, help the child figure it out.

Cardboard classroom analog clock

Take It Up a Level

Several times during the day, ask the children to tell you what time it is, and how much time there is before a certain activity on the announcement clock starts.

Schedule of Daily Events

Materials

18" x 12" sheet of construction (any color) in portrait position
pictures or photographs of daily events
clothespin

Math Objectives That Meet Standards

Children will:
1. Describe events by time of day.
2. Sequence events by duration of time.

How to Do It

- Make a daily schedule of activities on construction paper. Start with the arrival of the children at school and end with them leaving school.
- Hang the schedule on the back of the classroom door.
- On the schedule, record the times the children move to different activities during the day.
- Next to each time entry, put a photograph or picture of what is happening. For example, if the children are going to music, glue or tape a photograph of the children in their music classroom (or a picture of musical notes). If the children are moving from Group Time to centers, attach a photograph of the children in centers or a picture of center props (blocks, paintbrush, and so on).
- Make a 2" fold on the left edge of the schedule. This will allow the edge of the schedule to stick out so the "Leader of the Day" can attach a clothespin next to each activity entry the children are doing at the time as they move through their daily schedule.
- Put the schedule in a prominent place in the classroom.

Alarm Clock Time

Materials

alarm clock

Count on This

Give the children five minutes to move from one activity to the next. Set a clock. It helps.

Math Objectives That Meet Standards

Children will:
1. Measure time with an alarm clock.

How to Do It

- When the children are going to a special event, going to lunch, attending a "pull out" program in your classroom, or leaving at the end of the day, set an alarm clock to go off five minutes beforehand.
- When the alarm goes off, ask that the children stop what they are doing. This gives the children and you time for a less hurried transition to the upcoming activity or event. It also gives the children an understanding of time durations and the importance of completing tasks and activities in a specific amount of time.

The "What Happens Over Time?" Book

Materials

premade, blank-page book for
   photographs and class writings
camera
something to observe over time
   (such as a marigold plant)

In Addition

Listed below are events children
can observe and photograph or draw
over time:

- life cycle of a butterfly
- life cycle of a frog
- a puddle drying
- a block of ice melting
- grass growing in a controlled
   setting (winter rye seeds sprout
   fastest)
- changes in a compost heap

Math Objectives That Meet Standards

Children will:

1. Describe events by time of day.
2. Sequence events by duration of time.

How to Do It

- Suggest that the children do an observation project together—
   planting a flower perhaps, like a marigold, and watching it grow.
- Take photographs of the sequence of events. For example, plant a
   marigold seed and photograph the changes that take place each
   week.
- Put the photographs in the blank book.
- Ask the children to dictate or write their own notes describing the
   changes they observe. Add the writings to the book.

Take It Up a Level

Encourage the children to make their own book of their observations,
drawing the changes they see, and dictating or writing down what
happens.

Appointment Book

Materials

calendar (one per child)
crayons

Math Objectives That Meet Standards

Children will:

1. Name the days of the week and months of the year.
2. Sort and classify by categories (yesterday/today/tomorrow).

How to Do It

- This is an advanced activity for children who are ready to work at
   a higher level. Do this during Group Time or in another small group
   setting.
- Provide each child with a calendar.
- Ask them to make notations in their calendars about events. For
   example, challenge the children to mark the following:
   - birthdays
   - special school visitors
   - picture day
   - field trip day
   - the day that zoo-trip money is due
   - pet day
   - rainy days at school
   - library day

- If necessary, help the children find the days on the calendar.
- Once every two weeks, ask the children to use different colored crayons, three different colors to represent yesterday, today, and tomorrow, and color the boxes or rectangles that represent each day on the calendar.

The Wake-Up Chart

Materials

pocket chart
sentence strips with each child's name (one child's name per sentence strip)
laminator or clear contact paper

Math Objectives That Meet Standards

Children will:
1. Tell time to the hour, half-hour, and quarter-hour, using an analog or digital clock.
2. Identify a clock as a time-measuring instrument.
3. Describe events by time of day.

How to Do It

- Write each child's first name on a sentence strip and laminate it.
- Set up the pocket chart with different times, in 15-minute intervals, written along the right side of each line.
- As the children arrive in the morning, invite them to put their names next to the hour, half-hour, or quarter hour that they got up that morning. (**Note:** Leave some lines in the pocket chart blank so the children can write in the time they got up if the chart does not list that time).

The time I got up this morning was...

Hector	Wendy	Curt		6:15
Rachel	John	Sam	Lynn	7:30
Mike	Mia	Chris	Ki'	7:45
Laurie	Bryan	Jose		7:00
Maggie	Aaron	Tay		7:15
Kellie				6:30
Riley	Keisha			6:45

added by child ↗

Wake-Up Chart

Activities That Teach About Money

100-Day Celebration

Materials

100 pennies
100-day chart (18" x 18"
   construction paper)
glue
clear packing tape

Count on This

Encourage parents to get involved in fun projects with their children. The key word is *fun*!

In Addition

You can buy coins from other countries at flea markets and coin shops, or on the Internet. A good example is www.villagecoin.com.

Math Objectives That Meet Standards

Children will:
1. Sequence events by duration of time.

How to Do It

- Make a 100-box grid (10 boxes across and 10 boxes down) on a piece of 18" x 18" heavy construction paper. Number each box from 1 to 100.
- On the 100th day of school (the children can keep track using the School Year number line on page 58), have a "100 School Days Celebration."
- Kick off the event by making a 100-school-day penny chart during Group Time.
- Count the numbers 1–100 on the construction paper grid with the children and have them attach pennies under each number in the squares on the 100-box grid.
- Tape the pennies in place on the number line so the pennies stay on the number line for the entire school year.
- Put the construction paper grid on the wall above the number 100 on the School Year number line.
- Have the children follow up by finding 100 things at home and use them to make a chart at home that they bring to school.

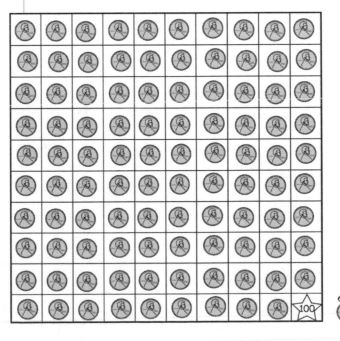

Penny-Date Progression Card

Math Objectives That Meet Standards

Children will:
1. Recognize coins.
2. Examine, manipulate, and identify familiar U.S. coins.
3. Sequence events by duration.

How to Do It

- Make photocopies of and set out the coin cutouts from the illustration on appendix page 166.
- Invite the children to match the dates to the dates on the cutout coins on the penny-date card (see illustration below). (This activity works well with younger children because it is interactive, and because the cutout coins are physically larger than real coins. This makes them easier for the children to handle.)
- Fold a long sheet of cardstock so it has several little peaks and folds, each fold deep enough to hold one of the coins and one index card.
- Copy the dates from the coins onto two separate sets of index cards.
- Glue the coins to the first set of index cards with matching dates.
- Glue the second set of dated index cards in chronological order to the date progression card.
- Invite the children to match and place the index cards with pennies and dates on them to the second set of dates glued in the folds of the date progression card.

Materials

sheet of cardstock
coin cutouts (see illustration on appendix page 166)
glue
scissors
marker
6" x 4" index cards

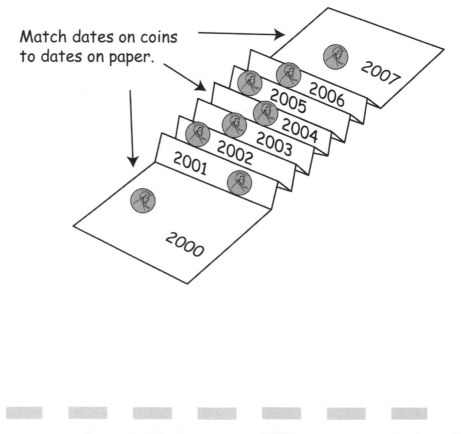

Match dates on coins to dates on paper.

"Jingle in My Pocket"

Materials

paper coins
craft sticks
small, brown paper lunch bags

Jingle in My Pocket

Math Objectives That Meet Standards

Children will:
1. Recognize coins.
2. Understand coin values.

How to Do It

- Copy the coin and dollar illustrations on this page, and attach them to craft sticks.
- Make Pocket Bags:
  1. Cut out the bottom section of a small brown lunch bag, so the children can reach through the bottoms of the bags and wave their stick coins out of the tops of the bags.
  2. Copy the pocket pattern (below) five times. Make one for each child to use.
  3. Cut out the pocket patterns and glue them to the lunch bags. Hand them out to each child.
- Have the children sing "Jingle in My Pocket," and push their coins through their pocket bags every time the song mentions the particular coins they are holding.
- Make one copy of the dollar for the leader to hold. After that, everyone will want one just like it.

Jingle in My Pocket by Sharon MacDonald
(Tune: "Short'nin' Bread")

Five pennies make a nickel.
Two nickels make a dime.
I can trade ten pennies for two nickels or a dime.
Jingle in my pocket, a dollar and a dime,
A penny and a nickel make me jingle all the time.

Two dimes and a nickel,
Make a quarter every time.
I can trade a quarter for three nickels and a dime.
Jingle in my pocket, a dollar and a dime,
A penny and a nickel make me jingle all the time.

Four quarters make a dollar,
Make a dollar every time.
I can trade four quarters for a dollar any time.
Jingle in my pocket, a dollar and a dime,
A penny and a nickel make me jingle all the time.

"Jingle in My Pocket" Chart

Math Objectives That Meet Standards

Children will:
1. Recognize individual coins.
2. Understand coin values.

Materials

poster board
markers
laminator or clear contact paper
images or copies of coins and of a
     dollar bill
hook- and soft-side Velcro squares
3" x 5" index cards

How to Do It

- Set up this activity in the Math, Music, or the Interactive Chart Center.
- Copy the "Jingle in My Pocket" song (on the previous page) on poster board and laminate it.
- Attach Velcro squares above all the places where coins or dollars are mentioned in the song.
- On index cards, write the names of all the monetary amounts mentioned in the song.
- Make copies of coin and dollar illustrations on appendix page 166.
- Apply the hook-side Velcro to the backs of the coin and dollar sketches, as well as the cards with the names of the money written on them.
- Challenge the children to match the index cards with the coin names on them to the coin names on the song chart, or match the coin and dollar drawings to their written names on the song chart.

"Jingle in My Pocket" Pop-Up Cards

Math Objectives That Meet Standards

Children will:
1. Explore the use and meaning of the dollar and the coin combinations that can be used to comprise the dollar.
2. Recognize the penny, nickel, dime, and quarter individually.

Materials

six sheets of colored paper
scissors
glue
coins (from the previous page)

How to Do It

- Make pop-up cards, as shown in the illustration on appendix page 167. You will need to make six different cards, with different-size cuts, for the different coin combinations mentioned in "Jingle in My Pocket."
- Make a pop-up card for each verse in the song, copying the words of the verse inside the card, below the pop-up cutout.
- Put the subject coin (a quarter, for example) on the card front and the coin combinations that make up the quarter (dimes and nickels, for example) on the inside of the pop-up cards.
- Invite the children to open the cards as they sing the song.

Piggy Bank Coin Counting

Materials

transparent (clear plastic) piggy
    bank (or a plastic mayonnaise jar)
coins

Math Objectives That Meet Standards

Children will:
1. Recognize coins.
2. Understand coin values.

How to Do It

○ Start this activity at the beginning of the year, if possible, with all the children gathered during Group Time.
○ Each day, put a penny in the piggy bank until there are five pennies.
○ When there are five pennies, take them out of the jar and help the children "discover" that the five pennies can be exchanged for one nickel.
○ After the second week, when there are five more pennies and a nickel in the piggy bank, take them out and count them.
○ Help the children discover that five pennies can again be substituted for a nickel and that two nickels can be substituted for a dime.
○ Put a dime in the piggy bank.
○ Repeat the sequence and substitution exercise through quarters and then, on the 100th day, substitute a dollar bill.

Coin Puzzles

Materials

five paper plates or five pieces of
    construction paper cut into circles
markers
construction paper or cardstock
coin pictures
glue
scissors

Math Objectives That Meet Standards

Children will:
1. Explore the use and meaning of currency and coins.
2. Recognize penny, nickel, dime, and quarter.

How to Do It

○ Follow the directions below to make puzzles, using the illustration below and the one on the following page as examples.
○ Set out five paper plates, or five pieces of construction paper cut into circles.
○ In the center of each circle or plate, put a coin: a nickel on one, a dime on one, and a quarter on each of the remaining three.
○ Draw a circle around each coin.
○ Around the center coin on each circle, put different coins whose values add up to the value of the coin in the center. For instance, for the nickel, put five pennies; for the dime, put a nickel and five pennies; for the first quarter, put two dimes and five pennies; for the second quarter, put five nickels; and for the third quarter, put two dimes and a nickel.
○ Spread the coins out on the circles so they have an even amount of space between them, and draw lines between the coins, from the circle drawn at the center to the paper's edge, so each section resembles a piece from a jigsaw puzzle.

- Cut out the pieces along the jigsaw lines, so in the end there are center cutout coins and several different puzzle pieces that have one coin on each.
- Put the puzzles pieces in the Math Center, and invite the children to solve them by putting the correct coins together around each circle cutout with a coin in the center.

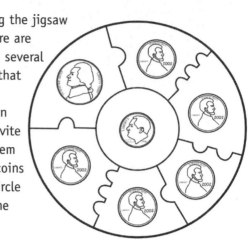

Hunt, Count, and Buy

Math Objectives That Meet Standards

Children will:
1. Explore the use and meaning of currency and coins.
2. Examine, manipulate, and identify U.S. coins.

Materials

Pigs Will Be Pigs by Amy Axelrod
play money

How to Do It

- The activity will be similar to the description in the book *Pigs Will Be Pigs* by Amy Axelrod.
- Before the children arrive at school, hide play money around the classroom.
- At Group Time, read *Pigs Will Be Pigs*. Carefully go over the menu pages in the book and let each child choose a meal.
- Write the menu selections on a chart, and then send the children on a money hunt.
- When the children finish gathering all the money, count it all to see if they have enough to buy all the meals they picked from the menu.

Coins Around the World

Materials

coins from countries throughout the
world, including the United States
tray
magnifying glass
globe (optional)

Math Objectives That Meet Standards

Children will:

1. Explore the equivalent value, similarities, and shapes of coins used throughout the world.

How to Do It

- At Group Time, place the coins on a tray.
- Invite the children to examine and compare coins from around the world.
- Discuss equivalent number values and list similarities and differences between the coins, such as shape, sizes, and color.

Take It Up a Level

On the globe, find the country where each coin is used. Ask the children to share what they know about the people in each country. Have a few facts ready to start the conversation.

In Addition

You can buy coins from other countries at flea markets and coin shops, or use search engines to find good sources on the Internet. A good example is www.villagecoin.com.

Coin Date Line

Materials

pennies with different dates put in
order by date (as many as your
class can put in order)
small container for the pennies
magnifying glass
tray

Math Objectives That Meet Standards

Children will:

1. Explore the use and meaning of coins, starting with the penny.
2. Examine, manipulate, and identify U.S. coins.
3. Recognize the penny.
4. Begin to categorize time intervals.
5. Sequence events by duration.

How to Do It

- This activity is an advanced activity. It will work best to introduce it during Group Time. After the children know how to do the activity, set it up in the Math Center.
- Set several different coins on a tray, along with a magnifying glass.
- Challenge the children to look at the dates on the coins using the magnifying glass, and put the pennies in order, from the earliest (smallest number) to latest (largest number) date.

Take It Up a Level

Add more pennies with more dates, and a variety of other coins for the children to sequence by date.

Geometry and Spatial Sense

CHAPTER 5

What Is ...?

Geometry deals with basic geometric shapes: the angles and proportions of the world around us. Shapes define our environment; they include the circle, triangle, square, rectangle, rhombus, and ellipse. We call these **plane** geometric shapes because they are two-dimensional (2-D), or flat. Flat things go on buildings, sheets of paper, and signs. Flat things also include things that have been squashed!

It is possible to combine geometric shapes to form other shapes. Triangles, for example, are the fundamental shapes of nature, with extensions like the diamond (two triangles) and the pentagon (five triangles).

There are three-dimensional (3-D) objects in geometry, called **solids**. A ball, for instance, is a good example of a solid. If a ball were really flat, it would be a circle. Children learn that a circle and a ball are related, but circles do not bounce.

Geometry also includes **points** and **lines**, which are introduced through maps and globes. Points and lines may not seem as interesting to children as other geometrical objects, but if the point is a place on the globe, it can be the most interesting thing a child could think about. And a line, well, a line goes on forever.

Angles and **curves** are interesting, too. An angle is the space between two lines that meet. A curve is a line that bends, or meanders, like a river. *Meander* is a great word for young children to learn. They can meander over to you slowly rather than coming over immediately, in a straight line. It is a word children enjoy learning and acting out.

Here are two more good geometric words to talk about: **congruency** and **symmetry**. Things are congruent when they match when one is placed on top of the other. Essentially, they are exact copies. Symmetry, on the other hand, suggests balance both to the mind and to the eye. Opposites are symmetric, for example, but they are not alike. One of the best examples of symmetry is front and rear silhouettes of the human body.

Symmetry

Young children are intuitively aware of symmetry. "Two-ness" is a primary expression of symmetry in that the second reflects the first. Two-ness puts things in balance. Nature abounds with twos: people have two eyes, two ears, two hands, and two feet. Many animals do, too. Twos are just about everywhere.

Around age five, children can identify and create shapes that have line and rotational symmetry. There is **line symmetry** in a peanut butter and jelly sandwich if you cut it in half and share one half with a friend. There is **rotation symmetry**—rotation around an axis—in a tricycle wheel that spins. In the classroom, rotational symmetry is reproduced when parquetry blocks are rotated around an axis through the center of a parquetry-block pattern.

To assess young children's understanding of geometric shapes, observe their activities and ask them questions:

- ◎ Can a child recognize shapes in the environment by name? Ask, "What shape is that?"
- ◎ Can a child pick out or point to specific shapes when the names of the shapes are said? "What in the room is the shape of a square?"
- ◎ Can a child identify other shapes similar to one initially indicated "Are there other shapes like that one? Which ones?"
- ◎ Can a child recognize a shape when it occurs in his constructions and designs? "What shape did you just draw? What shape did you make with the blocks?"

What Is ...?

Spatial sense is an awareness of one's relationship to other things in terms of *position* ("Where am I?"), *direction* ("Which way do I go?") and *distance* ("How near/far away am I?"). Spatial sense also involves organizing space so things fit appropriately for work and play, or the organization of objects to please the eye. Spatial-sense organization requires pattern recognition and the duplication and extension of patterns.

To examine a young child's spatial sense, observe and ask questions:

- ◎ Does a child use words that describe an object's/his/someone else's position, direction, and distance?
- ◎ Does a child respond to words about space in a way that shows understanding?
- ◎ Can she answer spatial questions? "Is it *under* the desk? See if you can get it."
- ◎ Does her block play show spatial awareness?
- ◎ Does the child move her body in space with awareness of others and their possessions/activities?
- ◎ Does her use of geoboards, parquetry blocks, color inch cubes, or pegboard show organization? Is organization improving with time?

Activities That Teach Basic Shapes

Geometric Shape Hunting

Materials

two or three brown paper lunch bags

Count on This

Use bags to limit what the children can collect. If you ask them to collect things without limiting the size, they are liable to return with jackets and shoes.

Math Objectives That Meet Standards

Children will:
1. Recognize, name, and describe basic shapes.
2. Identify shapes in the physical world.

How to Do It

- ○ Do this activity at any time during the day.
- ○ Make "shapes bags" by drawing different geometric shapes on 2–3 brown paper lunch bags and writing the names of the shapes below each of them.
- ○ When the children come into the classroom from lunch, return from outside play, or when they are on the way to center time, give a "shapes bag" to a few children. (Although only a few children get to do this activity at a time, repeat it over time until you give each child a bag.)
- ○ Ask the children to collect three objects from the classroom that are like the shapes on their bags, and put them inside the bags.
- ○ Close the bags when the children are finished and put them next to your chair or desk for sharing during Group Time.
- ○ During Group Time, invite the child who hunted down the three shapes to show them to the children. After Group Time, ask the children to return the items to the places they found them.

Take It Up a Level

Challenge the children to find the shapes in shapes. For example, ask the children "How many triangles and squares are there in a rectangle?" Extend and multiply shapes (Ask, "What can you make with three triangles? Four? Five?") Match, count, and make shapes. Shape a moment with shapes!

Name That Unit Block!

Materials

Unit Block Silhouettes and Names (see illustration on appendix page 168) posted in your Block Center

Math Objectives That Meet Standards

Children will:
1. Describe and compare real-life objects to geometric solids.
2. Build understanding of size as related to space.
3. Make connections between flat and solid forms.
4. Construct and sort solid shapes and forms.

How to Do It

- ○ Whenever you are near the Block Center, listen to what the children are saying and describing as they play.
- ○ Encourage the children to use the actual, geometric names of the blocks as they build.

Gel Geometry

Materials

small jar of thick hair gel
food coloring
resealable, quart-size freezer bag
clear packing tape
small chart paper
tray

In Addition

Many young children love to eat gel. Make sure you can see what is going on when you do this activity. If not, the children may remove the tape, unseal the bag, and try to eat some of the gel!

Math Objectives That Meet Standards

Children will:

1. Identify, describe, and draw plane (two-dimensional) geometric shapes.
2. Compare the sizes of geometric shapes.

How to Do It

- Put this activity in your Writing or Math Center but prepare the gel bag beforehand.
- Place ½ cup of gel in the freezer bag and add a drop of food coloring. Press the bag flat to push all of the air, not the gel, out of the bag.
- Tape the bag closed with clear packing tape and put it on the bottom half of the tray.
- Draw various shapes on a small chart. Laminate the chart and then attach it to the tray just above the baggie.
- Invite the children to make the shapes on the gel bags with their index fingers.
- As they draw, the gel moves out of the way, and the children can see the shapes they make. They can then smooth the shapes out with their hands and draw again.

Spongy Geometry

Materials

hot glue gun (adult only)
large rolling pin
circles, squares, rectangles, and triangles precut from craft foam or other spongy material
tempera paint
large metal or Styrofoam tray (the tray should be large enough to roll the rolling pin without bumping the tray sides)
easel-size paper sheets or precut sheets of butcher paper

Math Objectives That Meet Standards

Children will:

1. Recognize, name, and describe the basic geometric shapes.
2. Identify similar shapes in the physical world.

How to Do It

- This is an ideal activity for the Art Center. Remember to cover your worktable with newspaper. There will be some spills!
- Glue the shapes to the rolling pin, in any design, using hot glue. Make sure all of the shapes adhere firmly to the pin and there are no loose edges. (This is an adult-only step.)
- Pour a little tempera paint in the tray.
- Help the children roll the rolling pin through the tray, so the spongy shapes absorb the paint.
- Show the children how to roll the pin on paper until the shape images transfer over to the paper (see illustration).

Painting on Shapes

Materials

precut easel paper in the shape of
  circles, triangles, squares, and
  rectangles of different sizes
easel paper
tempera paint and paintbrushes
basket
paint-drying rack

Math Objectives That Meet Standards

Children will:
1. Recognize, name, and describe basic shapes.
2. Identify shapes in the physical world.
3. Compare the sizes of geometric shapes.

How to Do It

- This activity is ideal for the Art Center, but it captures the interests of math, science, and geometry avoiders, too!
- Put the precut shapes in a basket next to the easel.
- Set out the paints and brushes.
- Invite each child to select a paper shape on which to paint.
- When the children are finished painting, help them put their painted shapes on the drying rack.

In Addition

Put up signs on the display board that say: *Triangle, Circle, Square,* and *Rectangle*. When the paintings are dry, have the children suggest where to put up their paintings. Because the paintings are theirs, they will read the geometric shape signs!

What's the Shape?

Materials

white copy paper
crayons or markers
scissors

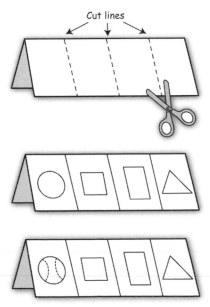

Math Objectives That Meet Standards

Children will:
1. Recognize, name, and describe basic shapes.
2. Identify shapes in the physical world.
3. Identify, describe, and draw plane (2-D) geometric shapes.

How to Do It

- Set up this activity in either the Math or Art Center.
- Fold white sheets of paper in half, lengthwise.
- Unfold the sheets and make three cuts, approximately equidistant, from the edge of the paper to the fold (do not cut beyond the fold).
- With markers, draw a circle, triangle, square, or a rectangle on each strip.
- Cut several other sheets of paper in the same way, and challenge the children to draw real-world objects on each of the four sections that match or resemble the shapes on the original strip.
- To help children who are struggling to learn shapes, set some shapes in a basket next to the activity so they can look at the shapes and examine them before attempting to draw them.

Take It Up a Level

Introduce two new shapes—the rhombus and the ellipse—and add them to the activity.

Rubbings of Shapes

Materials

circles, squares, triangles, and
  rectangles cut from medium-
  roughness sandpaper
white copy paper
peeled crayons
large tray
basket
Sticky Tack

Math Objectives That Meet Standards

Children will:
1. Recognize, name, and describe basic shapes.
2. Identify shapes in the physical world.
3. Identify, describe, and draw plane geometric shapes.
4. Compare the sizes of geometric shapes.

How to Do It

- Set up this activity in the Art Center.
- Put precut sandpaper shapes of different sizes in a basket, along with a stack of white paper and several peeled crayons.
- Invite the children to place the sandpaper shapes on the tray, place sheets of white paper over them, and rub the crayon back and forth until the shapes appear on the paper.
- If the shapes move while the children are rubbing, have them use a small ball of Sticky Tack to help hold them in place. When they finish, remove the Sticky Tack for future use.
- As the children use the shapes and explore them, engage them in conversations about the shapes.

Feeling Shapes in a Bag

Materials

several 3-D objects that together
  will fit in a large gift bag (ball,
  cube, triangular prism,
  rectangular prism, die, small
  triangular solid, a small ball, and
  a narrow rectangular box)
large gift bag with basic shapes
  drawn on the bag front (circle,
  square, triangle, and rectangle)

Math Objectives That Meet Standards

Children will:
1. Identify, describe, and draw plane (2-D) geometric shapes.
2. Find concrete objects in the environment that depict shapes.
3. Make connections between plane and solid shapes.
4. Sort solids and plane shapes.

How to Do It

- Prior to getting together for Group Time, put all the objects in the large gift bag.
- At Group Time, demonstrate the activity with one child.
- Ask the child to reach into the gift bag and feel one of the objects.
- Ask him to describe what he is feeling. For example, ask him to say the number of sides and the basic shape of the object.
- Challenge the other children to guess what shape the child is describing.
- After everyone guesses, ask the child to pull out the object so they can see what shape the child was describing.
- For a follow up, ask the child holding the shape to match it to the correct shape drawn on the front of the bag (see illustration).
- After the demonstration, set up this activity in the Math Center.

In Addition

Make up a traveling/waiting activity kit. These are activities to do with the children when you are traveling or waiting (for field trips, for the bus to arrive or stop, for parents to arrive).

CD Case Geometry

Materials

four or five clear CD cases with all the contents removed, including the CD tray

precut shapes of different colors and sizes (none larger than the CD case)

drawings of geometric shapes and real-life figures drawn from basic geometric shapes to insert in the CD case (see illustrations on appendix pages 169–171)

Math Objectives That Meet Standards

Children will:

1. Recognize, name, and describe basic shapes.
2. Identify, describe, and draw plane (2-D) geometric shapes.

How to Do It

- Make several 10¼" x 4½" CD covers, drawing shapes and real-life figures on both sides of the cover insert (see illustration on appendix page 169).
- Insert the covers into CD cases. This size is large enough that it will fold over in the CD case to cover both the front and rear panels.
- Put several precut geometric shapes in the CD cases (see illustration on appendix page 170).
- Divide the children into small groups working on the floor or at tables and give each group a CD case.
- Challenge the children to use the shapes inside the CD cases to make the shapes visible on the fronts and backs of the CD cases (see illustration on appendix page 171).

Take It Up a Level

Precut several pieces of 10¼" x 4½" paper, and invite the children to draw their own shapes and real-life figures for the cover and challenge the other children to make shapes to match the covers.

Geometric Shapes in Architecture

Materials

Architecture Counts by Michael Crosbie and Steve Rosenthal, or any book with photographs of architecturally interesting buildings

In Addition

Michael Crosbie and Steve Rosenthal have written several excellent architectural books: *Architecture Animals*, *Architecture Shapes*, and *Architecture Colors*.

Math Objectives That Meet Standards

Children will:

1. Identify, describe, and draw plane (2-D) geometric shapes and find concrete objects in the environment that depict shapes.
2. Make the connection between plane (2-D) and solid (3-D) forms.
3. Sort solids and plane geometric shapes.
4. Recognize the characteristics of solids and geometric shapes, including curves, angles, and lines.
5. Recognize symmetry and congruency in architectural forms.

How to Do It

- Share this book featuring photographs of architecturally interesting buildings with the children during Group Time. *Architecture Counts* is particularly good because it combines shapes and counting.
- Discuss each picture and the shapes in each photograph.
- Challenge the children to point out the many photographs containing *combined* geometric shapes, such as rectangles and squares in windows and doors.

Take It Up a Level

Ask older children to describe the shapes they're seeing: "Do the shapes have curves? How many lines are in the shapes? Are they symmetrical? How many angles can you count?"

Neighborhood Walk

Materials

neighborhood with a few interesting buildings

camera (a digital camera would be ideal)

In Addition

Set up a "Museum of Neighborhoods" in the school hallway, against the wall, so everyone in school can enjoy the children's work and learn more about shapes.

Math Objectives That Meet Standards

Children will:

1. Identify, describe, and draw plane (2-D) geometric shapes and find concrete objects in the environment that depict shapes.
2. Make connection between 2-D and 3-D shapes.
3. Sort solid shapes and forms.
4. Represent commonly used fractions (½) (¼) (⅓).

How to Do It

- Take the children on a walk through the neighborhood, asking them to look for geometric shapes on buildings.
- Photograph the shapes the children find. Take a photograph, for example, of the rectangular door, the triangular gable-end of a roof, a square window, window panes, and similar structures. Public buildings often have some of the most interesting shapes.
- After returning from the walk, display the pictures on an "Our Neighborhood Walk" bulletin board for a few weeks so the children can review their walk, talk about the shapes they found, and find new shapes that they had not noticed before while on the walk.

Neighborhood Walk Tab Book

Materials

photographs from the previous activity, "Neighborhood Walk"

cardstock

notebook rings

scissors and glue

white copy paper

hole punch

Math Objectives That Meet Standards

Children will:

1. Identify, describe, and draw plane geometric shapes and find concrete objects in the environment that depict shapes.
2. Make connections between 2-D and 3-D shapes.
3. Sort solid and geometric shapes.

How to Do It

- Make cardstock cutouts of the tab patterns using the illustrations on this page and the next as examples.
- Cut several pieces of white paper to fit between the cardstock cutouts. Do not include the tabs when you cut the tab pages from the white paper.
- At two points along the edge of all the pieces of cardstock, as well as the sheets of paper, punch binder holes.
- Insert the cardstock and paper cutouts in the notebook and close the rings. On each cardstock's tab, draw a different shape: circle, square, triangle, and rectangle.
- During Group Time, show the children the tab book and discuss the shapes drawn on the tabs. Remind the children about the neighborhood walk and the pictures of the different geometric shapes the children found during the walk.
- Ask the children to decide which shapes on the tabs in the shape book most resemble the shapes in each picture.
- When they finish sorting all the photographs by shape, help the children glue them to the sheets of paper in the proper sections of the book.

○ The tab book will be of high interest to the children, because they took the walk and worked on it together. Put it in the Library or Math Center for the children to review for as long as they show interest.

Take It Up a Level

Encourage the children to make their own tab books, sort photographs by shape, and glue them into their tab books.

Shapes in the Neighborhood

Materials

low-sided box, approximately 18" x 24", for each child

many square and rectangular boxes, spools, film canisters, containers, milk cartons, and paper cups (all of which fit in the low-sided box with room to spare)

glue

In Addition

The younger children's constructions may not look like neighborhoods, but doing this activity starts them down the path toward representational thinking as they begin to consider how shapes best fit in the spaces available for them.

Math Objectives That Meet Standards

Children will:
1. Identify, describe, and draw plane geometric shapes and find concrete objects in the environment that depict shapes.
2. Make connections between 2-D and 3-D forms.
3. Sort solid shapes and forms.
4. Compare sizes of geometric shapes.
5. Recognize basic properties of, and similarities and differences between, simple geometric shapes.
6. Recognize the characteristics of curves, angles, lines, congruence and symmetry.

How to Do It

○ This activity works well in the Art Center.
○ Set a low-sided box top out in front of every child.
○ Invite the children to use smaller boxes, containers, cartons, and other shapes to build "neighborhoods" in their low-sided box tops.
○ Help the children glue the shapes together as they create the buildings and the details of their neighborhoods (see illustration).
○ These neighborhoods the children create offer unique and interesting opportunities to talk about shapes. For instance, ask the children how shapes come together to make other shapes, and how shapes are alike and different.

What Shapes Do You See?

Materials

easel paper and markers
paper
crayons

Count on This

Children are always lining up in groups to walk somewhere. These times can sometimes be frustrating for children. Having activities planned in advance will help structure the time and make for happier transitions.

Math Objectives That Meet Standards

Children will:
1. Make connections between 2-D and 3-D shapes.
2. Sort solid (3-D) and plane (2-D) shapes.
3. Compare the sizes of geometric shapes.

How to Do It

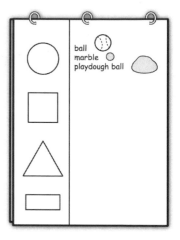

- Start this activity with a demonstration during Group Time, and then move it to the Library or Math Center.
- Make a chart of a large circle, square, rectangle and triangle on easel paper, with the shapes on the left side, as shown in the illustration.
- Put up the chart on the inside of the front door or near it.
- When the children are lining up to go somewhere as a group, or when there is a free minute or two, point to one of the shapes on the easel paper, and ask the children to identify an object in the room that has a similar shape.
- Jot down some of their ideas on the chart.
- If time allows, give the children markers, crayons, and paper, and ask them to make illustrations of the objects they added to the chart.

Take It Up a Level

Challenge the older children to write the names of the objects the class identifies and then illustrate the shapes on the easel paper.

The "I Spy Shapes" Game

Materials

one sheet of cardstock for each child in your room (use various colors)
access to a laminating machine or clear contact paper
scissors
black marker
basket

Math Objectives That Meet Standards

Children will:
1. Recognize, name, and describe basic shapes.
2. Identify shapes in the physical world.
3. Identify, describe, and draw plane (2-D) geometric shapes.
4. Compare the sizes of geometric shapes.

How to Do It

- Draw and cut out circles, squares, triangles, and rectangles from cardstock, making each shape about the size of a sheet of copy paper. Laminate each shape twice.
- Put the shapes in a basket and set the basket next to front door.
- This next time the children need to line up to go somewhere, ask them to do so a few minutes ahead of time.
- Ask a child to pull the shapes from the basket and put them in a straight line, going toward the door.

In Addition

During otherwise idle time, like when the children lining up to go somewhere, do activities that build on the subjects the children have been learning. If you are studying shapes, for example, find a way to use them more widely in everything you do. Playing go-out-the-door games is one of the best ways to do it. This activity is a good example.

- Choose any of the ways listed below to use the shapes, or invent new ways of your own:
  - Ask each child to go to a shape he names.
  - Ask each child to go to a shape, then name it.
  - Ask each child to go to a shape and call another child to line up behind him on another shape.
  - Ask each child to go to a shape and name a 3-D object in the classroom that resembles that shape.
  - Ask each child to go to a particular shape based on the other people and shapes around it. For instance, ask a child to go to the shape that is behind Sara, in front of the square.
  - Distribute the shapes to each child before lining up to go out the door.
  - Ask the children to make a pattern of shapes in a line going toward the door. For example: circle, circle, square, square, circle, circle, square, square. Then, try triangle, triangle, rectangle, rectangle, and so on.
- After the children understand the game, ask a child to call out the line-up pattern.

How to Eat Geometry

Materials

"O"-shaped cereal, round crackers, bagels, thin-sliced pickles, apples, zucchini, and tomatoes

square and rectangular crackers and cereals

triangular crackers and cheese and deli meats cut into triangles of various sizes

Math Objectives That Meet Standards

Children will:
1. Recognize, name, and describe basic shapes.
2. Compare the sizes of geometric shapes.

How to Do It

- Ask the children to decide as a group what geometric shapes they would like to eat for snack, based on the shapes of the food available.
- When they eat, challenge the children to name and talk about a characteristic or two of the shapes they are eating.
- Serve snacks of various shapes and let the children tell you the shapes they are eating. Discuss how they knew (for example, "What does a square taste like?").

Cookie Cutter Shapes

Materials

cookie cutters in geometric shapes
playdough
plastic tray

Math Objectives That Meet Standards

Children will:
1. Recognize, name, and describe basic shapes.
2. Compare the sizes of geometric shapes.
3. Sort solid (3-D) and plane (2-D) shapes.

How to Do It

○ Help the children use cookie cutters to cut shapes from playdough. Work on a plastic tray.

○ Encourage the children to put the pieces together edge to edge, like a puzzle, to make other shapes.

○ Encourage them to talk about what shapes they are cutting out and the shapes they are assembling to make other shapes. Ask the children to describe the characteristics of the different shapes. For example: The square has four corners and four sides. The sides are the same length. The triangle has three points and three sides, and so on.

Straw-and-Pipe-Cleaner Shapes

Materials

drinking straws cut in halves and fourths
pipe cleaners

Math Objectives That Meet Standards

Children will:
1. Recognize, name, and describe basic shapes.
2. Compare the sizes of geometric shapes.

How to Do It

○ The Art or Math Center is a great place for this activity.

○ After demonstrating the activity during Group Time, put the straws and pipe cleaners in a basket and let the children make geometric shapes with them by sliding the straws over the pipe cleaners and folding the pipe cleaners to make different geometric shapes.

○ To complete the shape, they twist the two pipe cleaner ends together (a good exercise for fingers).

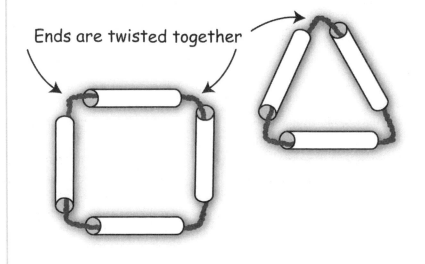

Ends are twisted together

Making Playing Card Suits

Materials

deck of playing cards with all of the face cards removed

math stand (see appendix page 164) four to five of each geometric shape made in "CD Case Geometry" on appendix page 170 (use different sizes of shapes)

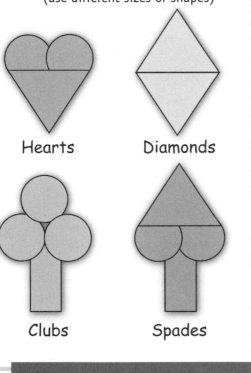

Hearts   Diamonds

Clubs   Spades

Math Objectives That Meet Standards

Children will:

1. Identify, describe, and draw plane (2-D) geometric shapes.
2. Compare the sizes of geometric shapes.
3. Recognize, name, and describe basic shapes.

How to Do It

- This is a great activity for children to do in small groups.
- One at a time, display a card from each of the four suits in a deck of cards. Start with hearts.
- Ask the children how they can make a heart from the basic shapes they know, and then ask them to make a heart from those shapes. (If they do not say "triangle and circles," guide them toward those answers by talking about the shape of a heart.)
- Give each child a triangle and two circles, or give the children several shapes, and ask them to pick up a triangle and two circles from the shapes they already have.
- Ask the children to explain how the shapes can form a heart. As they describe the steps, draw a picture of the shapes forming a heart, as shown in the illustrations. Be sure to include the overlapping edges of the shapes in the drawing, so the children see how to place the shapes over one another.
- After mastering hearts, challenge the children to make diamonds, clubs, and spades out of various geometric shapes.
- Continue until the children finish making all the shapes.

Geoboards

Math Objectives That Meet Standards

Children will:

1. Identify, describe, and draw plane (2-D) geometric shapes.

How to Do It

- Display the geoboard and geometric-shaped pattern cards in the Math Center.
- Put the rubber bands in one basket and the pattern cards in another.
- Invite the children to select pattern cards and attempt to duplicate them on the geoboard.
- When they finish, ask the children to remove the rubber bands and return them to the basket.

Materials

geoboard

rubber bands of different colors and sizes

sample shape pattern cards (see illustrations on the next page)

two baskets

In Addition

Children love rubber bands. They love to pull and stretch them and a few of them will shoot them at each other. Don't ignore this behavior. Instead, have frequent safety lessons in safe rubber band use. Rubber bands are wonderful tools for developing the small muscles of small hands and fine-tuning children's fine motor development. We want the children to use them safely.

Take It Up a Level

Challenge the older children to design their own pattern cards and challenge friends to duplicate the shapes on a geoboard.

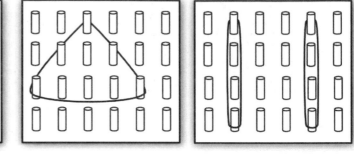

Frame-a-Shape Game

Materials

frame made from heavy construction paper, or overhead film frame
geometric shapes cut from different colors of cardstock that fit the frame
bulletin board at child's height

Count on This

Make changes. Try new things. You never know which activities will grab the children's interest and spur them on to new things.

Math Objectives That Meet Standards

Children will:
1. Identify, describe, and draw plane (2-D) geometric shapes.
2. Compare the sizes of geometric shapes.
3. Recognize, name, and describe basic shapes.

How to Do It

○ Put cardstock shapes up on the bulletin board in random order.
○ Demonstrate the activity in a small or large group setting by giving a child the frame and saying:

Play the Frame-a-Shape game.
Put a _____ (circle, square, triangle, rectangle) in the frame.

○ Consider adding color to the shape description. For example, say, "Put a green circle in the frame." The colors may help some children find the correct shapes.

○ As the children become more proficient identifying shapes by name, begin asking them to put the frame around the shapes based on the number of sides they have.
○ Hang the game frame next to the shapes so the children can play Frame the Shape with their friends.

Activities That Teach Spatial Sense

Build in a Box

Materials

box from the grocery store with low sides (canned goods box)
blocks

Count on This

Children are drawn to block play. When they play with blocks in a box, it adds interest and builds skills.

Math Objectives That Meet Standards

Children will:
1. Interpret spatial sense: position, direction, distance, and order.
2. Create structures using 3-D shapes.
3. Understand and describe position, direction, and distance.
4. Build understanding of size related to space.

How to Do It

○ Place the box in the Block Center.
○ Encourage the children to use the blocks to build objects and structures within the low-sided box.
○ Ask the children about their structures, and about how they placed the blocks to fill their areas most successfully.

Classroom Photograph Puzzle

Materials

digital camera
step ladder
glue and scissors
sheet of cardstock
resealable plastic bag

In Addition

Let the children climb the ladder one step at a time, with you supervising each climb, so each child gets to see the room from the camera's view. The ladder climbing will be the hit of the day. **Safety Note:** Never let a child use a ladder without an adult providing close and careful supervision.

Math Objectives That Meet Standards

Children will:
1. Understand and describe position, direction, and distance.
2. Interpret space: position, direction, distance, and order.

How to Do It

○ Stand on a three-step ladder and take photographs of eight contiguous sections of your classroom.
○ Print and trim them so you can put them together to make a complete photograph of the whole room.
○ Glue the photographs on cardstock and cut them into puzzle pieces. Laminate the pieces and put them in a resealable plastic bag for storage. Set out the plastic bag and challenge the children to put the classroom puzzle together.
○ Encourage the children to talk about where the different landmarks of the room are located on the puzzle.
○ Set this activity up in the Games and Puzzles Center. Keep it there until the children lose interest.

Take It Up a Level

Help the children to photograph the room on the step ladder. If photographing is not feasible, have them draw the room from camera's-eye view. This is an early exploration of mapping.

"Up and Down"

Materials

blocks (one per child)

In Addition

After the children learn the opposite words, make puppets to use with the song. Set out several magazines and catalogs and encourage the children to tear out images that represent opposites. Photocopy the illustrations, and cut each one out separately. Match the opposite actions, and glue them to brown paper lunch bags, putting one image on the bottom of the bag, and its opposite inside the flap, so when a child puts his hand in the bag and closes it into the flap, one image is visible, and when he opens it, the opposite image is visible (see illustrations below).

Math Objectives That Meet Standards

Children will:

1. Understand and describe position, direction, and distance.
2. Interpret space: position, direction, distance, and order.
3. Build an understanding of size as related to the space that contains it.
4. Use geometric vocabulary such as *near/far, close/far away, up/down, beside/next to*.

How to Do It

○ This activity works best in Group Time, but you can do it with groups of three or four children, too. It's fun.

○ Write "Up and Down" on a chart in large print. Sing or chant "Up and Down" with the children.

Up and Down by Sharon MacDonald
from the *Watermelon Pie and Other Tunes*! CD

*Up and down are places
That I'm supposed to know;
Just like in and out,
Off and on, and high and low.*

*But I've noticed when I get there,
All tired and out of breath,
There's just another up and down
To other places left!*

*Up and down, high and low,
Off and on, fast and slow,
Back and forth, big and small,
Here and there, short and tall.*

○ After the children learn the song, have them pick up their blocks and follow the movements in the song with them, moving the blocks around as they sing. For example, the children would move the block up and down on their stomachs and chests, and in and out of an arm with the hand placed on the hip, following the directions in the lyrics.

Geometric Words in Block Construction

Materials

unit blocks

Math Objectives That Meet Standards

Children will:
1. Construct and sort solid shapes and forms.
2. Understand and describe position, direction, and distance.
3. Use the vocabulary of geometry.

How to Do It

- Introduce this activity during Group Time, with two children assisting. Once the children are familiar with it, move it to the Block Center.
- Using words like *over*, *under*, *around*, and *behind*, have one child tell another how to build a structure, describing where each block should go.
- When the first child finishes giving directions, have the children switch roles.

Obstacle Course

Materials

classroom space
footprints cut out from paper
copy or easel paper
Sticky Tack
basket

Count on This

Simple activities linked with physical movement are great for young children and lots of fun for them to do. These activities take surprisingly little time and they do not require lots of preparation, especially when you ask the children to give you a hand.

Math Objectives That Meet Standards

Children will:
1. Understand and describe position, direction, and distance.
2. Use the vocabulary of geometry (*through*, *under*, *around*, *behind*, and *over*).

How to Do It

- Pair up the children and have them make footprints:
  - One child stands on a piece of paper, while the other one traces around both his feet.
  - Have the children switch places and repeat the footprint tracing.
  - The children cut out their own footprints and put them aside until all of the children's footprints are ready.
- Set up an obstacle course trail in your room using the paper footprints. Use tables for the children to go *through*, and *under*, a carpet square to walk *around*, a block wall or partition to walk *behind*, and yarn to jump *over*.
- Use Sticky Tack to stick the footprints to the floor, marking the trail through the obstacles. Give each child a turn to go through the course.
- Store the footprints in a basket and put away the obstacles.
- The next time, challenge the children to make an obstacle course (when there is time to do it).

Doll Furniture in the Block Center

Materials

doll furniture
blocks
magazine photographs of rooms in
  houses

Math Objectives That Meet Standards

Children will:

1. Construct and sort solid shapes and forms.
2. Understand and describe position, direction, and distance.
3. Use the vocabulary of geometry (*through, under, around, behind,* and *over*).

How to Do It

- Set out doll furniture in the Block Center, and invite the children to use it to recreate the interior designs they see in magazines.
- Challenge the children to describe where they are putting the furniture and why.
- Encourage them to rearrange the furniture often.

Where Are You?

Materials

children in your room

In Addition

Laughter is a great relationship builder, so use silly positional commands with the children:

- Sit on your toes *in front of* the wall.
- Look *back*, put one hand *next to* your ear and walk *backward* to the table.
- Crawl *under* the carpet square and *over* the chair seat, touch the *top* of your shoe.

Math Objectives That Meet Standards

Children will:

1. Understand and describe position, direction, and distance.
2. Use the vocabulary of geometry (*through, under, around, behind,* and *over*).

How to Do It

- Do this activity anytime during the day, especially when you have a few minutes to spare.
- Direct the children to move to different places in the classroom and perform different actions in each of them. For example:
  - Stand beside the table that is behind Larry.
  - Sit beneath the table that Larry is sitting on.
  - Stand behind Susan, in front of Larry.
  - Walk beside Larry and beside Susan.
  - Stand on the carpet square in the Games Center next to Larry, in front of Susan.
- When the children get to the place you describe, ask them to say aloud where they are.
- When the children learn to play the game, let them take turns giving directions.
- As an alternative, don't tell the children where to go, just walk several of them to a location of your choosing and ask them to use positional words to tell the class where they are.

"Shuffle, Bend, Slide, and Wave"

Materials

lyrics to "Shuffle, Bend, Slide, and Wave" written on a chart
scrunchie (one per child)

Count on This

Movement is important to the development of children's spatial skills. Because young children learn best by moving, the "Shuffle, Bend, Slide, and Wave" gives children the chance to learn positional words while they move their bodies.

Math Objectives That Meet Standards

Children will:
1. Understand and describe position, direction, and distance.
2. Use the vocabulary of geometry; left and right.

How to Do It

- During Group Time, teach the children the lyrics to "Shuffle, Bend, Slide, and Wave."
- Put a scrunchy on each child's left wrist to identify which direction he moves first when singing the song.
- Sing or chant "Shuffle, Bend, Slide, and Wave" with the children, inviting them to act out the movements the song describes.

Shuffle, Bend, Slide, and Wave by Sharon MacDonald
From the *Jingle in My Pocket!* CD

Shuffle to the left and shuffle to the right,
And you snap, and snap, and snap, and snap.
A heel and a toe and turn yourself around,
And a heel and a toe and, on you go!

Bend to the left and bend to the right,
And you clap, and clap, and clap, and clap.
A heel and a toe and turn yourself around,
And a heel and a toe and, on you go!

Slide to left and slide to the right,
And you stomp, and stomp, and stomp, and stomp.
A heel and a toe and turn yourself around,
And a heel and a toe and, on you go.

Wave to the left and wave to the right,
And you walk, and walk, and walk, and walk.
A heel and a toe and turn yourself around,
And a heel and a toe and, sit back down.

Sorting, Classifying, Graphing, Data Analysis, and Probability

CHAPTER 6

What Is ...?

Sorting means separating. To be able to separate, a child must recognize similarities and differences. The simplest form of sorting is **matching**. A simple set of objects to match are socks. Matching socks is fun. Socks are familiar.

What Is ...?

Classifying means grouping. To be able to group, a child must recognize similar attributes or characteristics among various objects. Grouping socks with holes in the toes separate from those with no holes in the toes makes sense to young children. Holes are familiar.

What Is ...?

An **attribute** is a quality an object or person has, like color, shape, size, height, flavor, texture, or odor. In this book, *attribute* and *characteristic* mean the same thing. Children learn to sort and classify by attributes.

If children can't sort and classify, they may not be able to match the right shoe to the correct foot when they get dressed in the morning. They might get stuck academically, too, unable to understand graphing, analyze data, or work with concepts of chance, like probability. Reading may prove difficult, too, for a child who does not recognize patterns. Most children are born capable of pattern recognition, the mental process of sorting and classifying. If children are asked, however, to graph before they can match, sort, classify, and recognize by attributes they will not be able to do it and they may have difficulties at later points in their early education.

There are seven distinct levels children move through in learning to sort. Children must progress through them at their own speed:
1. Child matches by a highly dissimilar characteristic:
"Find the pair of boots (among sandals)."
2. Child matches by a similar characteristic:
"Find the tennis shoes that match."
3. Child sorts by one attribute (such as color):
"Put the red shoes here and the white ones there."
4. Child sorts by two attributes (color and closure):
"Separate the red shoes with laces from the blue shoes with Velcro."

5. Child classifies by function:
"Are these shoes for work, play, or dress up?"

6. Child classifies by what does not belong:
Given an assortment of objects, the child figures out which one is different from the others. For example, given an assortment of shoes like that found on appendix pages 172–173, the child can determine the following:

- sandals don't belong because they have a buckle;
- bedroom shoes don't belong because they do not have a bow;
- a loafer doesn't belong because it has a penny;
- a cowboy boot doesn't belong because it has a spur;
- flip-flops don't belong because they go between the toes; and
- ballet slippers don't belong because they are the only ones shown together in a single image.

7. Child classifies by multiple attributes. Children sort by color, closure, function, and size. The children's perspective and explanations matter, as in step 6 above, because there are a number of acceptable answers, depending upon each child's point of view.

Sorting becomes more difficult for children as the number of attributes increases, or as the attributes become more similar. How objects are sorted depends on the perspective of the child. Flip-flops, for instance, are for work when lifeguards use them, but for everybody else, flip-flops are for play. Interpretation and perspective count.

What Is ...?

Graphing is a way to show two or more comparisons visually. With the teacher's encouragement, for example, the children might want to discover the different kinds of shoes the children are wearing. To find out, the children can take off their shoes, count the different kinds, and display their findings on a Shoe Bar Graph (see illustration on appendix page 174).

When children make graphs, they are using several skills, such as sorting, classifying, counting, comparing, and measuring. As the children improve these skills, they often want to compare more than two items, and create more permanent records of their findings, such as classroom wall charts. Once the children start making graphs, they often think of ways to use them on their own.

Bar and **picture graphs** are the most typical graphs children use in preschool and kindergarten. **Line graphs** are introduced in First Grade. The first graphs children learn should be horizontal **bar graphs** that display number data ascending *left to right*. Data displayed vertically should show numbers ascending bottom to top.

Lists and *tallies* provide a place for the children to organize information before graphing it.

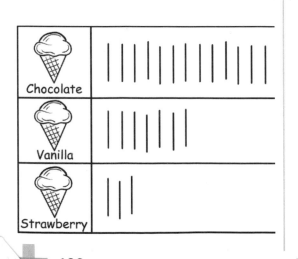

What Is ...?

Data analysis is the interpretation of accumulated information. For example, if the children want to discuss the most popular shoes in the class, they will need to collect data on all the different types of shoes everyone is wearing.

What Is ...?

Probability looks at the outcome of an event and determines whether it is likely or unlikely. For example, is it likely or unlikely that most of the children will wear the same shoes tomorrow?

It is best to introduce young children to graphing, data analysis, and probability by using real objects from their everyday lives. Shoes are a good example, but there are many others. Children can sort shoes into a shoe bag (see illustration on the left) or match them in a horizontal real-object bar graph. The children can graph other objects from their everyday world, for example: seeds, buttons, apples, crayons, paper clips, dog biscuits, hair color, blocks, stickers, pompoms, pets, and so on.

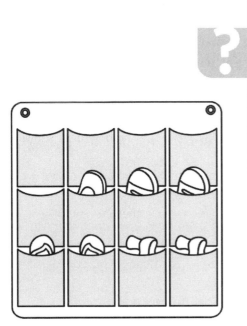

What Is ...?

A **Venn diagram** is a visual tool that helps group objects that share some, but not necessarily all, characteristics. The basic form consists of two overlapping rings. While more complex Venn diagrams exist, it is best to wait until later elementary grades to introduce these to children.

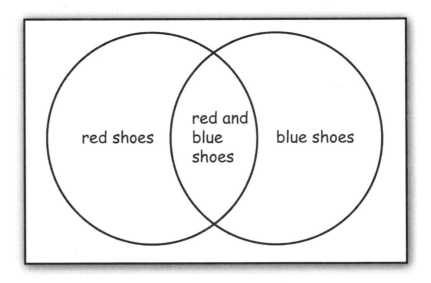

Venn diagram, *What Color Are Your Shoes?*

A graph is a powerful way to organize, compare, and record information visually. That is why it is important for young children to learn to use graphs, and to interpret the information they contain.

Activities That Teach Sorting, Classifying, Graphing, Data Analysis, and Probability

Which Shoes Do You Choose?

Materials

12–15 illustrations of various shoe types (see illustrations on page appendix pages 172–173)

crayons

cardstock

snack-size resealable bags

glue

scissors

laminator

Math Objectives That Meet Standards

Children will:

1. Sort and classify materials by one or more characteristics.
2. Compare and contrast objects.
3. Sort and classify real objects, and pictures of objects, and explains how sorting was done.

How to Do It

- If you plan to work in groups of three to four children, you will need one set of all the shoes from the illustration on appendix pages 172–173 for each group. Store each paper cutout shoe set in a resealable plastic bag.
- If you pair the children, make a set for each pair.
- Make extra sets for independent work for children working in your classroom at a higher level.
- Color the shoes with crayons to make them easier to sort and more fun to work with (the brain loves color!).
- Use the crayons to:
  - Color the hiking boots, loafers, cowboy boots, and sandals *brown*.
  - Color the flip-flops, bedroom shoes, and rain boots *red*.
  - Color the ballet shoes *pink*.
  - Color a pair of tennis shoes *red, white* and *blue*.
  - Color a second pair of tennis shoes *white*.
- Glue each page you color to cardstock.
- Cut out each shoe and then laminate it (it is a lot of work, but it is worth the time). Make an overhead of the shoes and cut them out.
- In Group Time, start by having a discussion on the characteristics children can use to sort shoes, and then sort the shoes by a highly dissimilar characteristic. After that, move through the sorting levels as discussed in the introduction to this chapter.
- After you have a clear sense of the level at which your children function, try pushing them to sort at the next hardest level. For example, try the "what-does-not-belong" level.
- These discussions and debates offer excellent chances to build trust and collaboration and to use descriptive math words.
- As you find the levels that individual children are working at, create groups of three or four children who have similar skills and work on sorting shoes using the overhead.

Materials

lyrics to "A Barefoot Walker's Shoes"
(can be used as a poem)
chart paper
marker

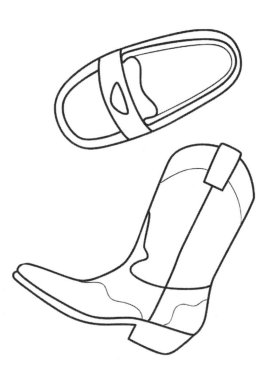

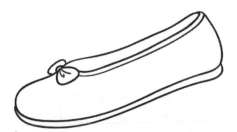

Math Objectives That Meet Standards

Children will:
1. Sort and classify objects by one or more characteristics.

How to Do It

- Teach the children "A Barefoot Walker's Shoes" as a song or poem.
- After the children learn the words, encourage them to act out the movements they describe.
- Let the children decide how they should look doing the movements. They can hike, swim, climb, dance, ride, slide, and so on—this is a great time for them to express their creativity.

A Barefoot Walker's Shoes by Sharon MacDonald
(from the *Jingle in My Pocket* CD by Sharon MacDonald)

I have shoes I use for hiking,
Flippers I wear to swim.
And tennies that grip me tightly,
So I can climb the jungle gym.
I have ballet dancing shoes,
Boots I wear to ride.
And shoes I use for skating,
So I can roll and slide.
I have plastic boots for snow,
Floppy rubber ones for rain.
And sandals just for skipping
With my friends who skip the same!
Beneath my bed are flippers,
Slippers, boots, and shoes.
"What do I like to wear?"
"Barefoot is what I choose!"
What'll I do with my shooooooes?

- Repeat the verse with the children, changing the ending to *"Don't wanna use my shooooooes!"*
- During Group Time, have the children decide the function of each pair of shoes mentioned in the song.
- Make a list of different shoe functions on a sheet of construction paper:
  - Boots are for hiking.
  - Cowboy boots are for riding horses.
  - Ballet slippers are for dancing.
- Encourage the children to classify the shoes in groups, such as all the boots, all the slip-ons, or all the shoes with laces.

Take It Up a Level

After the children learn the song and are familiar with the different types of shoes, give them sheets of paper, crayons, and markers and ask them to make drawings of things the song mentions, or to design their own boots and shoes.

The Mixed-Up Pompom Sort

Materials

27–36 red, yellow, and blue, small, medium, and large pompoms mixed up in a big bowl or basket tray separated into nine parts with colored tape (see illustration)

Count on This

Have several sample carpet squares for the children to pick for sitting on at different times of the day. Children stay put longer, learn more, and are happier on carpet squares that they select for themselves! I have no proof but my own experience and observations. It seems that way because young children have so few choices, they respond well to the ones they get to make. I wish I would have known that earlier in my teaching career, it would have saved me hundreds of hours!

Math Objectives That Meet Standards

Children will:
1. Sort and classify objects by one or more characteristics.
2. Compare and contrast objects.

How to Do It

- Set up this activity in the Math Center.
- Ask the children to sort the pompoms into the sections on the tray by color and size.
- Ask the children to explain to friends how they sorted the pompoms on the tray, such as in the following ways:
  - two large red ones in one section,
  - two large blue ones in another,
  - one large yellow pompom in one,
  - three medium blue ones in another,
  - four medium red in another,
  - five medium yellow ones in one,
  - two small red in a section, and
  - six small yellow and five small blue ones, all in the last section.

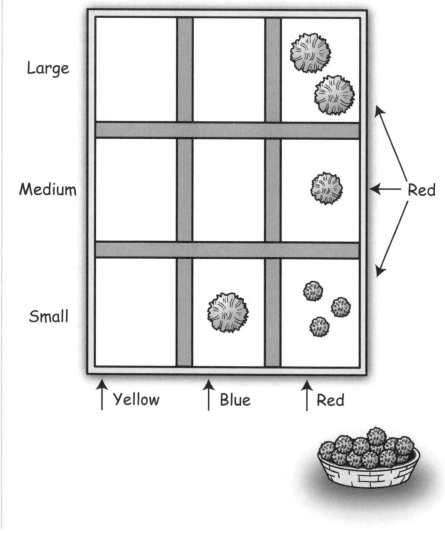

The Button Box

Materials

The Button Box by Margarette S. Reid and Sarah Chamberlain

box filled with an assortment of buttons

Count on This

In the Math Center, keep the number of buttons to 30–35. Too many choices can cause confusion and frustration. Lots of button choices do work well in Group Time, though. If you pair the children to work, have 10–20 buttons for each pair of children.

When you move the activity to the Math Center, have a different button project each week.

In Addition

A sorting tray is useful because it keeps the activity organized. Here are some button-sorting examples:

- Sort all the four-hole and two-hole buttons.
- Sort all the red, blue, and orange buttons.
- Sort the metal and the cloth buttons.
- Sort all the round, square, and rectangular buttons.
- Sort all the plain and the fancy buttons.
- Sort all the wooden and metal buttons.
- Sort all the buttons with holes in the shanks and the buttons that have holes through the buttons.
- Sort the shiny and the dull buttons.
- After doing these, challenge the children to think up some of their own ways to sort.

Math Objectives That Meet Standards

Children will:
1. Sort and classify materials by one or more characteristic.
2. Compare and contrast objects.
3. Sort and classify using real objects, or pictures, and explains how the sorting was done.
4. Collect and organize data about themselves, their surroundings, and meaningful experiences they have had.

How to Do It

- Before you read the book during Group Time, talk to the children about buttons.
- Have them look at their clothes. Ask them, "What are buttons used for?"
- Tell a story, or two, about buttons. For example:

  Francis I, King of France (1494-1547), lived during the early Renaissance, about 500 years ago. He had more than 13,600 gold buttons on a single uniform and, for a short time, he ordered that no one could have buttons on their uniforms or clothes except him. Imagine! Everyone's blouses and shirts flew open and their pants fell down! Rich noblemen and women wore the biggest, prettiest, and fanciest buttons that were available in the world.

- Read *The Button Box* to the children over a period of several days. There is a lot of information about buttons and much for the children to do.
- After you read a few pages, pull out the box of buttons and ask the children to find buttons like those described in the pages they read.
- Ask them to sort the buttons, and talk about why they sorted them the way they did, asking them, for instance, what characteristics they used to group the buttons.
- Continue this activity until the children finish the book completely.
- Put the box of buttons and *The Button Box* in the Math Center for the children to explore.
- When the children have had plenty of time to explore the buttons, use them to teach the children to count, sort, match, and graph.

Take It Up a Level

Challenge the children to sort 30–35 buttons at one time and tell you what characteristics they used to sort the buttons (they can have as many as 10–12 different piles of buttons).

Button Graph

Materials

30 sheets of graph paper with 1" x 1" grids on them

buttons

Math Objectives That Meet Standards

Children will:

1. Sort and classify materials by one or more characteristics.
2. Compare and contrast objects.
3. Construct graphs using real objects, or pictures, to answer questions.
4. Interpret and use information from graphs.

How to Do It

- Set out graph paper for the children.
- Use 15–20 buttons from the previous activity and show the children how to graph the buttons using different characteristics of them.
- Write the first characteristics across the bottom of the graph paper.
- Show the children how to select buttons to match the characteristics you picked.
- After they understand how to graph, put the children in groups of three to four and have them repeat the activity, choosing their own set of characteristics by which to sort the buttons.
- After selecting the characteristics, help the children make legends across the bottoms of their own sheets of graph paper.
- Put the buttons within reach of the children and put the graph paper in the middle of their work area.
- Encourage the children to select their buttons based upon the characteristics they identified, and then place them in the first squares on their sheets of graph paper.
- As the children select other buttons and put them in other squares in their graph sheets based upon the characteristics they selected, encourage them to work from left to right, and bottom to top.
  Note: Each group's graph may be different.
- When the children have an understanding of how to graph, set up this activity in the Math Center for the children to explore on their own. They may "group up" to do the activity or work independently.

Take It Up a Level

Challenge the children to draw versions of their graphs on paper.

Crayon Color Bar Graph

Materials

crayons
bar graph sheet

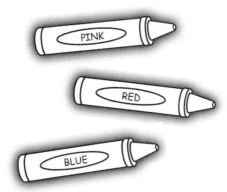

Math Objectives That Meet Standards

Children will:

1. Sort and classify materials by one or more characteristics.
2. Compare and contrast objects.
3. Construct graphs using real objects, or pictures, to answer questions.
4. Interpret and use information from graphs.
5. Collect data in an organized way.

How to Do It

- ○ Do this activity with groups of three to four children.
- ○ Give each child three or four crayons.
- ○ Encourage the children to examine each crayon and count the number of letters in the name of each color (for example: *red* has 3 letters; *green* has 5).
- ○ Then, ask the children to put the crayon next to the correct number on the graph, as shown in the sample graph on appendix page 175.
- ○ After the children understand how to do this activity, set it up in the Math or Library Center or for the children to explore independently.

Weather Graph

Materials

weather graph (see illustration on appendix page 176)
crayons
weather

Count on This

It doesn't cost much to use things in the natural world to teach! You can build an entire early childhood curriculum around weather, rocks, trees, grass, colors, rainbows, day and night, water, and people, to name just a few "natural" materials.

Math Objectives That Meet Standards

Children will:

1. Investigate, identify, and describe different forms of data collection, such as recording daily temperature and weather conditions.

How to Do It

- ○ Talk with the children about weather conditions. Describe what a legend is (a "key" to the symbols and colors used in a graph).
- ○ Make a legend for a weather graph. Ask the children what colors they think indicate sunny, rainy, cloudy weather, and so on. Use drawings of different weather events, too.
- ○ Create a Weather Graph, putting the drawings of different weather types vertically on the left side of the graph, and then making a grid, with one slot for every day of the month to the right of each weather type.
- ○ Each day, choose a child to color the correct weather column using the appropriate color, based on the earlier discussions the children had about which colors go with different types of weather.
- ○ At the end of the month, count the number of sunny, cloudy, windy, rainy, and icy days and total them on the right end of the graph.

Take It Up a Level

Collect weather data for an entire year. At the end of the year, make a graph showing the number of each kind of weather in every month, using the same legend as that in the main activity.

Whole Body Graph

Materials

king-size bed sheet
permanent marker
children

In Addition

Ideas that the children might
suggest include graphing:
- color of eyes
- number of pockets on clothes
- type of pet (dog, cat, gerbil, horse, rabbit, fish or no pet)
- color of shoes
- shoe type (slip-on, tie, or buckles)
- length of hair
- favorite food (pizza, spaghetti, chicken, hamburgers)

When the activity is over, fold up
the sheet and keep it accessible.

Math Objectives That Meet Standards

Children will:
1. Sort and classify objects by one or more characteristics.
2. Compare and contrast objects.
3. Construct graphs using real objects or pictures to answer questions.
4. Interpret and use information from graphs.

How to Do It

- Do this activity during Group Time and use it whenever you have time on your hands during transitions.
- Draw 1' square grids on a bed sheet.
- The first time you do this activity, choose an attribute for the children to graph on the bed sheet. For example, ask the children to line up on the graph according to hair color.
- Ask a child to stand in one square across the bottom of the grid. For example, in square one, put a brown-haired child; in square two, put a blonde-haired child; in square three, put a black-haired child. Ask the children to line up behind the child who has the same color hair as they do.
- After the children are able to do this quickly and easily, let them decide on the attributes by which they want to graph themselves.

Photo Graphs

Materials

4" x 6" full-length photo of each
child
old window shade
basket
cardstock
glue
scissors
permanent marker

Math Objectives That Meet Standards

Children will:
1. Sort and classify objects by one or more characteristics.
2. Compare and contrast objects.
3. Construct graphs using real objects, or pictures, to answer questions.
4. Interpret and use information from graphs.

How to Do It

- Find an old window shade at a flea market or garage sale. While old window shades are getting harder to find, they are worth the search. You can use a window shade all year long for graphing activities, and a window shade is easy to store.
- Draw a grid of 6" x 8" rectangles on the shade in permanent marker.
- Take full-length photos of all the children. Glue the photographs to cardstock, cut them out and laminate them.
- Store the photos in a basket.
- Place the shade on the floor and challenge the children to use the photographs to make a graph based on the sorting of characteristics similar to those used in the previous activity, "Whole Body Graphs."

Cube-Me Graph

Materials

half-pint milk cartons (two for each child)
white construction paper
glue
tape
scissors
window-shade graphing grid
Styrofoam peanuts

In Addition

Ask parent volunteers and upper-grade children to help make the Cube-Me cubes for the younger children who cannot make them.

Math Objectives That Meet Standards

Children will:
1. Construct graphs using real objects, or pictures, to answer questions.
2. Interpret and use information from graphs.
3. Collect and organize data about themselves, their surroundings, and their meaningful experiences.

How to Do It

○ As a group, ask the children to select six attributes about themselves, such as eye color, hair color, foot size, height, favorite pet, and so on.
○ Help each child make a cube from two half-pint milk cartons (see illustrations and instructions below).

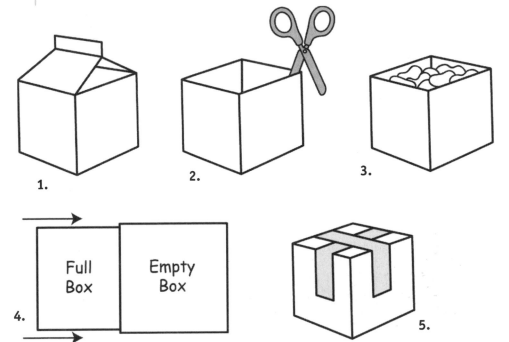

1. Cut the top off each carton.
2. On one carton, cut down 2" along each edge, so the second box will fit easily.
3. Fill the cut-corner box with Styrofoam peanuts.
4. Slide the empty box inside the full box.
5. Seal the cube with tape and cover it with paper or contact paper.

○ Help the children find and cut out or draw a picture of each attribute they named, and glue one to each of the six sides of the cube. The cube provides characteristics for six days of graphing.
○ Each day, have the children vote on one characteristic they want to graph that day, such as hair color.
○ Write the names of each of the children's hair colors along the top of a sheet of construction paper, tape it to the wall, and invite the children to stack their cubes below the names of their hair colors.

Bag a Graph

Materials

one large gift bag (approximately 12" x 18")
hook- and soft-side Velcro sticky dots
permanent marker
cardstock
copier paper
glue
scissors

Count on This

Children love activities in bags. I think it is because they get to look inside!

Math Objectives That Meet Standards

Children will:

1. Construct graphs using real objects, or pictures, to answer questions.
2. Interpret and use information from graphs.
3. Collect and organize data about themselves, their surroundings, and their meaningful experiences.

How to Do It

- Draw a graphing grid on a gift bag, like the one in the illustration below.
- Make a legend at the bottom of the bag to display the attributes the children will be graphing. The legend in the illustration below, for example, shows different hair colors.
- Title the bag at the top and affix hook-side Velcro dots in each section of the grid.
- Make title strips for all of the attributes the children will graph, laminate them, and drop them in the bag.
- Write the children's names on copy paper and cut out the names.
- Glue each name to cardstock and affix soft-side Velcro sticky dots to the back of each nametag.
- Store all of the children's names, as well as the attribute titles, in the bag.
- During Group Time, ask the children which attribute they want to graph: eye color, hair color, favorite pet, favorite color, favorite food, and so on.
- Write the title of the graph on a paper strip, affix Velcro sticky dots and attach it to the bag.
- Have the children remove their names from the bag and attach them to the Velcro dots in the appropriate attribute column.
- Demonstrate this activity during Group Time, and then move it to a graphing area in the Math Center.
- Leave the bag in the Math Center and let the children decide for themselves what attributes they want to graph, either in small groups or as individual projects.

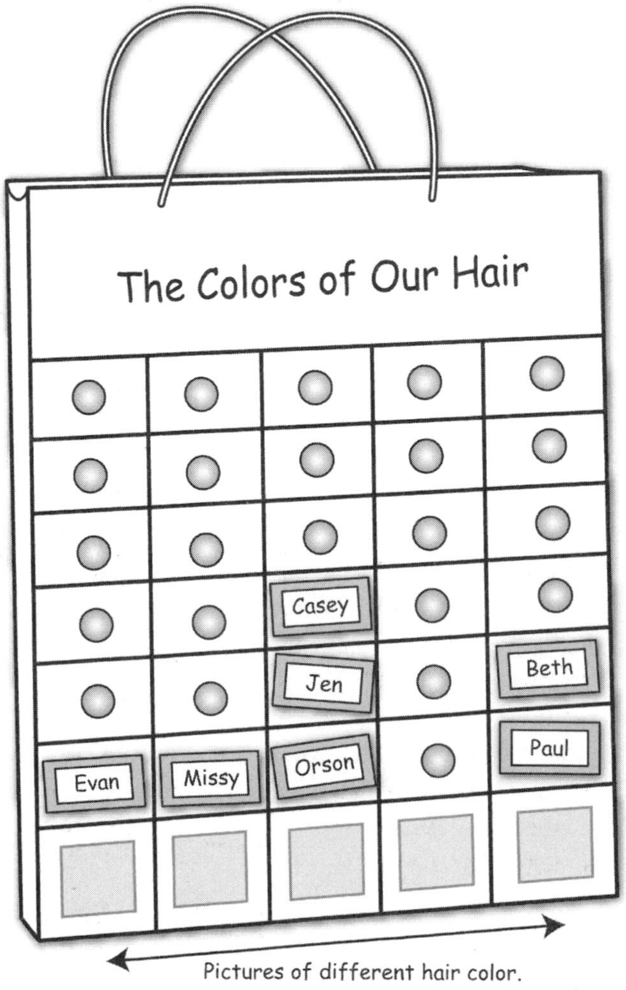

The Colors of Our Hair

Pictures of different hair color.

Yes-and-No Graph Bag

Materials

gift bag
long strips of hook-side Velcro
sticky dots of soft-side Velcro
cardstock and white paper
permanent marker
glue
scissors

In Addition

Here is a list of yes-and-no preferences:

- ○ I am a girl (boy).
- ○ I have black hair (blonde, brown, red).
- ○ I have on a short sleeved shirt.
- ○ My hair is curly (straight, combed, brushed).
- ○ I sleep on my back.
- ○ I like stories about people (animals, insects, cartoons).
- ○ I have laces in my shoes.
- ○ I can skate (skip, gallop, hop, leap).
- ○ I can ride a tricycle (bicycle).
- ○ I can jump rope (throw, rope).
- ○ I can sing.
- ○ I can dance.
- ○ I like spaghetti (other foods).
- ○ I can swim.
- ○ I have a window in my room.
- ○ I know everyone's name in the room.

Math Objectives That Meet Standards

Children will:

1. Sort and classify objects by one or more characteristic.
2. Compare and contrast objects.
3. Construct graphs using real objects, or pictures, to answer questions.
4. Interpret and use information from graphs.
5. Collect data in an organized way.

How to Do It

- ○ Introduce the Yes-and-No Graph during Group Time.
- ○ Draw a vertical line down the center of a large gift bag with a permanent marker.
- ○ Draw a horizontal line near the bottom for the yes-and-no legend.
- ○ Draw a horizontal line near the top for the title of the graph.
- ○ Make "Yes" and "No" signs and back them with cardstock (see illustration below).
- ○ Make a bunch of bag title signs, enough to change them every week throughout the school year.
- ○ Write all of the children's names on white paper, glue them to cardstock, and cut them out.
- ○ Put soft-side Velcro dots on the back of each name card.
- ○ Explain that when they come in each week they will go to the graph, read the sentence at the top, such as "I like spaghetti," and put their name in either the "Yes" or "No" column. If the children are not able to read, suggest that they ask another child or help them read the sentence.
- ○ Store all of the children's names and bag titles in the bag.
- ○ When the children come in each Monday, ask them collectively to choose one yes-or-no statement to put on the graph bag.
- ○ Once the children pick a yes-no statement, attach it to the top of the bag and invite the children to come up to the bag, one at a time, find their nametags, and place them on either the "Yes" or "No" side of the bar graph.

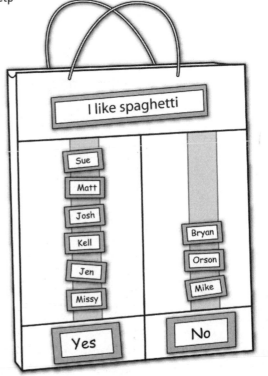

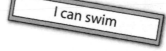

A Year of Graphs

Materials

1" three-ring binder
box of sheet protectors
cardstock
white copier paper

Math Objectives That Meet Standards

Children will:
1. Sort and classify materials by one or more characteristics.
2. Compare and contrast objects.
3. Construct graphs using real objects, or pictures, to answer questions.
4. Interpret and use information from graphs.
5. Collect data in an organized way.

How to Do It

- ○ Use the binder to save all the graphs the children make at Group Time throughout the school year.
- ○ Make up the binder before the school year starts so you can start filling it from the very first day.
- ○ Ask the children to come up with a title page for the book of graphs. For example: "Graphing Throughout the Year," "A Year of Graphs," or "A Bunch of Graphs."
- ○ Insert a cardstock sheet in the sheet protectors, so they can each hold two graphs.
- ○ When the children complete a graph together, help each of them transcribe the graph onto white paper and slide it into one of the sheet protectors.
- ○ Date each graph, to keep them in sequence for the year.
- ○ Store the binder in the Math Center so the children can review all their data collections and their progress in graphing.

Take It Up a Level

After the children understand how to transcribe the graph to copy paper, let them transcribe the graph themselves and put the graphs in the binder, in chronological order.

Venn Diagram Shoe Sort

Materials

large gift bag
several doll shoes
blue and yellow markers
crayons

Math Objectives That Meet Standards

Children will:
1. Sort and classify real objects or pictures, and explain how the sorting was done.
2. Investigate, identify, and describe various forms of data collection.
3. Collect and organize data about themselves, their surroundings, and their meaningful experiences.

How to Do It

- ○ Take out a large gift bag. Set it out so its bottom flap faces down, and draw two overlapping circles on the bag front (see the illustration on the next page).
- ○ Draw one circle with blue marker, the second circle with yellow.
- ○ Use crayons to color the circles. Use green where the circles overlap.

Count on This

A Venn diagram is a tool to help young children find the similarities and differences among objects and to notice the many ways that objects are similar and different. What you find depends on the characteristics or attributes you are looking for. They do not "do" anything with the information. Using Venn diagrams helps the children build a foundation for later stages of learning that depend on the children's ability to notice now how things are alike and different.

In Addition

Do other Venn diagram groupings or comparisons:

○ Two animals, people, or dolls— for example, animals with brown fur, animals with white fur, and animals with brown and white fur

○ Two plants (types of bushes, two flowers)—for example, red flowers, yellow flowers, and flowers that are both colors

○ Frogs and toads—for example, characteristics of frogs and toads that are the same (four legs/two eyes/eat insects) and characteristics that are different for each animal (toads live in dry places and frogs live in wet places, frogs can swim and toads cannot, frogs lay eyes in the water and toads do not)

○ Zoo and farm animals—for example, list animals that are found on a farm but not at a zoo, animals that are found at the zoo but not on a farm, and animals found in both zoos and on farms

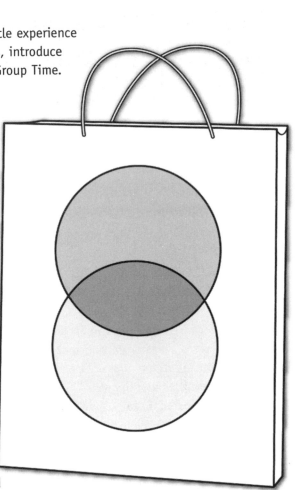

○ For children with little experience using Venn diagrams, introduce the activity during Group Time. For children with experience using Venn diagrams, put all the doll shoes in the gift bag and place the activity in the Math Center.

○ Each time you change the attributes by which the children match, sort, or group the shoes, demonstrate how to do it during Group Time.

○ Challenge the children to sort the shoes on the Venn diagram based on whether the shoes are for work, play, or both; to sort based on size and color; or to sort based on whether the shoes are inside shoes, outside shoes, or both.

Take It Up a Level

Extend the Venn diagram construct by asking the children to group themselves physically by characteristics, such as those who have blue eyes from those with brown hair, or those who have birthdays in the summer from those who like ice cream. Fine tune their choices to help them group themselves in overlapping circles.

Coin Flip Tally

Materials

large gift bag
white copier paper
duplicated copies of both sides of
    pennies (heads and tails)
pencil
small paper bag
penny

In Addition

Children who do the coin-flipping activity many times often find that the results are different every time. At one time, children in my classroom posted 53 tally sheets with different results on the class bulletin board as evidence. After that, none of the children had a preference for who called which side of the penny or when they did it. They became casual about it. You could say they became fatalistic flippers because they knew that there were no guarantees for a winning flip!

Math Objectives That Meet Standards

Children will:
1. Investigate, identify, and describe various forms of data collection.
2. Compare and contrast objects.
3. Collect data in an organized way.
4. Count and tally information from familiar experiences.

How to Do It

- In an active classroom, some problems require a coin flip to settle differences. It is the easiest and fairest solution to many conflicts. Coin flipping often is not so simple anymore, however, because most children want an edge; they want to know which side of the coin comes up most often! In my experience, children often think that heads will come up more often because it is "heavier" than the tails side of the coin.
- Put the penny in a snack-size plastic bag, and put the plastic bag inside a gift bag.
- Make several copies of a tally sheet, like the one in the illustration below. Cut them apart and put them inside the gift bag, along with a pencil.
- Challenge the children to flip the coin 12 times and record the results on their tally sheets (see appendix page 177).

Jug Tally

Materials

two plastic half-gallon plastic
    milk jugs
scissors
small basket
Velcro
6" x 2" strips of colored cardstock
paper clips

Math Objectives That Meet Standards

Children will:
1. Investigate, identify, and describe various forms of data collection.
2. Compare and contrast objects.
3. Count and tally information from familiar experiences.
4. Collect data in an organized way.

How to Do It

- Cut off the tops of the two milk jugs.
- Wash the jugs and remove the labels.
- Attach a 6" strip of hook-side Velcro to the milk jugs, vertically, along the centerline of each jug (see illustration on next page).
- Cut name strips for each child and have or help the children write their names on the strips.

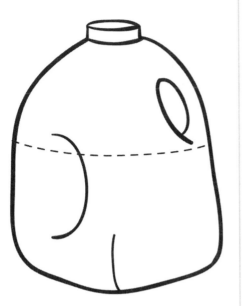

- Put all of the name strips in the small basket.
- Explain to the children that the jug tally is a "choice," or yes/no activity.
- Make different activity titles on cardstock and attach them to the jugs using soft-side Velcro. For example, the first titles used on the jug might be "I like Water Best" and "I Like Milk Best."
- Place the jugs beside the door. At the end of the day, as the children are heading out the door, ask them to put their name strips in the jug that has the title card with the statement with which they agree, depending on their preference for milk or water.
- When the children return the following morning, choose two children to sort the data from the two jugs. Give them paper clips to attach every five strips together from each jug.
- Ask the two children to report their findings about how many children prefer milk and how many prefer water. The differences in preferences may surprise several of the children.
- Every few days, re-title the activity so the children can make new choices. Other ideas to use for jug tally titles are:
  - I like using a crayon/I like using a marker.
  - I like apple juice best/I like orange juice best.
  - I like to play in sand/I like to play in grass.
  - I like to swim/I like to bike.
  - I have been to a lake/I have been to a river.
  - I like to play inside best/I like to play outside best.
  - I like to bring my lunch/I like the cafeteria food.
  - I like frozen yogurt/I like ice cream.
  - I like hot weather/I like cold weather.
  - I have a long name/I have a short name.

Patterns and Number Relationships

CHAPTER 7

What are ...?

Patterns are sequences that repeat. The simplest one is ABAB. Patterns are all around us, in the natural displays and configurations we see, like the sediment layers in an exposed hillside, or in the numbers we use. Often, the closer we look, the more patterns we find. It is important for young children to look for and to recognize patterns.

Why Is Pattern Recognition Important?

Recognizing patterns is essential to critical thinking and prediction. If the brain finds a pattern, prediction is possible. Without patterns, solutions are merely guesses or retrievals from memory. If a young child cannot see the pattern, she cannot predict what happens next. For example:

○ "What's next (in the daily routine)?"
○ "What number is after two?"
○ "Complete the sequence: large wood block, large nail, small wood block, small nail; large wood block, ___size nail?"
○ "Complete the table setting: plate, glass, knife, fork and spoon; plate, glass, _____, _____, _____?"
○ "If I wear _____ size shoe and it is too small, what size is next?"

What are ...?

Number relationships are the inherent patterns in numbers. For example, our base-ten number system is full of patterns. The two most basic are one, two, three, and so on, and 10, 20, 30, 40, and so on. Young children learn what is next in each series and how to figure out what comes next.

The same is true with skip counting. Skip counting is a number-relationship pattern. Two examples are 2, 4, 6, 8, 10, 12, __? and 5, 10, 15, 20, 25, 30, __? What comes next?

In our base-ten system, the number "10" is a special counting "bridge" that repeats in a pattern: 10s are saved and ones are accumulated. There are nine ones (one to nine); when you run out of ones another 10 is added and you start counting ones again. For example: one, two, three, four, five, six, seven, eight, nine, 10 plus one, 10 plus two, 10 plus three, and so on. Young children learn to accumulate the ones and a few 10s. We save the rest of the numbers for the later grades of school!

Using Nesting Cups

○ Nesting cups are wonderful to use for hands-on, patterning activities for three- and four-year-olds. A set of eight cups put in order by size, smallest to largest, for example, teaches *seriation*. *Seriation* is the arrangement of objects or numbers in a pattern.

○ Early childhood classrooms work with standard and nonstandard measurements. Nesting cups illustrate standard measurement because the system for putting them together, and taking them apart, resides within the cups themselves. On the other hand, when the children put themselves in order by size, shortest to tallest, they are using nonstandard measurement and they are also learning seriation patterning skills.

Looking for Patterns

We want young children to search for patterns in their surroundings and to recognize the patterns in numbers. This searching brings meaning to seemingly random events and provides a way for children to interpret and to think about what they see.

Pattern recognition skills give children a means by which to explain and make sense of events. Pattern seekers are successful learners and persistent problem solvers. They learn that recognizing patterns helps them find answers. When children have developed pattern recognition skills, their minds move flexibly from the whole to parts of the whole and back again easily. This freedom of thought makes the accommodation of new information easier for them.

When children reach this developmental stage, they choose preferred or favorite ways to put things together. For example, a child may need to see a whole pattern first to understand its nature, or a child may prefer to see the parts and then assemble the whole from them.

Mathematics is the study of patterns. As young children's learning evolves, patterning skills are extended to more and more observations that can be expressed in pattern "codes," such as ABABCABABC. The mind reads the code and understands not only that code, but the future expressions of similar codes as well.

Patterning skills teach young children to recognize, describe, match, complete, extend, and create patterns. The same is true when they match, sort, and group by attributes, and learn to recognize geometric shapes. These activities provide the ground work for patterning skills. Patterning skills are prealgebraic skills, too.

Pattern recognition activities should start on the left and move to the right, just like standard English text. As you teach children a pattern by placing objects in an AB order, for instance, be sure to speak the pattern, too, as you place the objects.

After the children understand the AB pattern in horizontal form, move to vertical AB patterns. Moving to vertical can be a challenge for children because the eyes and brain prefer working along the horizon. Scanning the horizon for food or danger is how humans evolved, so horizontal is easier.

PINK   RED   BLUE   YELLOW

Levels of Pattern Recognition Skills

1. Child recognizes grossly **dissimilar** patterns of real objects. If you set up an ABAB pattern (pumpkin, apple, pumpkin, apple) and ask a child, "What do you see?" The child is able to describe the pattern correctly.

2. Child recognizes AB patterns of real objects that are **similar**, like shoes. If you set up an ABAB pattern of shoes (tennis shoe, sandal, tennis shoe, sandal), the child can match the pattern.

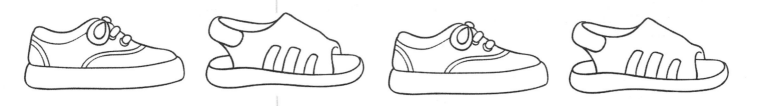

3. Child **extends** simple patterns. In the ABAB shoe-pattern example above, the child continues the shoe pattern without clues or verbal help.

4. Child **creates** a pattern. This is the level at which we want children to work. Working with shoes, for example, children are able to make their own AB patterns based upon characteristics they select.

The activities that follow will help you build pattern recognition skills into the natural setting of your classroom. That means you won't have to change what you are doing, just recognize the opportunities that emerge naturally from what is going on already. The less contrived the activities, the more effective they will be.

Activities That Teach Patterning Skills and Number Relationships

Snap, Clap, Snap, Clap

Materials

pattern cards (duplicate the cards on appendix page 178)
cardstock

Count on This

When children challenge a friend with movement pattern cards, they come up with some fancy patterns. The child being challenged will work very hard to repeat the patterns. Many of the children enjoy the competition, while others may get frustrated. Frustration usually means that they are trying to work at too high a level. Encourage them to be successful at another level with another child working at that level.

Math Objectives That Meet Standards

Children will:
1. Reproduce patterns using sound and physical movement.
2. Use patterns to predict what happens next.
3. Replicate patterns.

How to Do It

- This is a great activity to do when you have five minutes to spare or when you are transitioning to cleanup time.
- Start snapping and clapping. See if the children pick up on it. Initially use the pattern ABABAB.
- Speak the words and add body movements: "Clap, stomp, clap, stomp, clap, stomp," or "Head, shoulder, head, shoulder, head, shoulder," touching the body parts as you say the words.
- Encourage the children to come up with their own AB word patterns with corresponding movements. They can create some really interesting ones.
- After the children can do AB patterns, expand to ABC and then, ABCD.
- When the children understand the movements, make cards like those shown in the illustration on appendix page 178. Cut out, laminate, and glue them to cardstock.
- Put the cards in the Math Center. Invite the children to copy and extend the patterns or create their own patterns with the cards, or to share and copy each other's patterns, which is a lot of fun for them!

 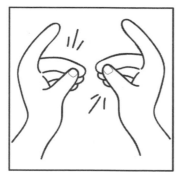  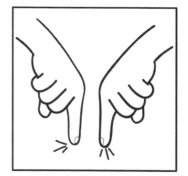

Boy, Girl, Boy, Girl Pattern Game

Materials

no materials needed

Math Objectives That Meet Standards

Children will:
1. Recognize patterns in the physical world.
2. Recognize, describe, extend, and create a variety of patterns.

How to Do It

- This is another good activity to do when you are on the way somewhere or when you have a few minutes to spare.
- Ask the children to line up to play the boy-girl pattern game.
- Explain the game and start by calling out, "Boy, girl, boy, girl," moving down the line to touch each child on the shoulder.
- As an alternative, call out the children's names, "Michael, Mary, Sam, Susan, Victor."
- Ask the children to name the pattern.
- Shape your activities for the patterns you want to make. For example, use hair colors of red, brown, blond, and black for ABCDABCD patterns. Make a pattern based on clothes pockets of none, two, and five for ABCABC patterns.
- When the children understand the pattern game, let each child be a caller of the game.

Outside Patterns

Materials

Lots and Lots of Zebra Stripes by Stephen R. Swinburne (or a similar book with photographs of patterns in nature)
chart paper and marker
paper and crayons or markers
digital camera (optional)

Math Objectives That Meet Standards

Children will:
1. Recognize patterns in the physical world.
2. Recognize, describe, extend, and create a variety of patterns.

How to Do It

- Share *Lots and Lots of Zebra Stripes* with the children during Story Time.
- Extend the activity for several days by spending lots of time with each page. The photographs in the book show cactus spikes, insects, watermelons, zebras, sunflowers, vegetables, the beach, and cross-sections of fruit.
- Each page is an invitation to find patterns. Talk about what patterns are, and how they repeat themselves in the natural world. There are also many opportunities to talk about patterns as geometric shapes. Some of the patterns in the photographs will be hard for the children to find, so they will have to focus.
- Later, before the children go outside, read the book to them again and then ask them to look for patterns on the playground and school grounds.
- Keep a running list of patterns they find.
- After they come inside, help them add the patterns to a list kept on the classroom wall. Encourage the children to make drawings of the patterns they saw.
- If possible, every now and then, use a digital camera to photograph a pattern that may be gone in a day or two, like a flower or a butterfly.

Inside Patterns

Materials

children moving through different
    environments
clipboard and pencil
chart paper and markers

Math Objectives That Meet Standards

Children will:
1. Recognize patterns in the physical world.
2. Recognize, describe, extend, and create a variety of patterns.
3. Use patterns to predict what comes next.

How to Do It

- This is a good activity to do when you are walking with the children, especially down the halls and through different parts of the building.
- Challenge the children to look for patterns in the carpet, wallpaper, wall paintings, tile floor, windowpanes, room numbers, table arrangements, colors, ceiling lights, sounds heard, gym floor, gym pads, and in the cafeteria line.
- Write the patterns that the children find on a clipboard to record the data-gathering process.
- As individual children learn to write, have them share the responsibility of recording the patterns observed.
- Transfer the data to a chart in the classroom for the children to illustrate.
- Put up the chart next to the outdoor pattern chart from the previous activity, "Outside Patterns." Using the companion charts leads to interesting comparisons and discussions.

Calendar Patterns

Materials

morning Group Time calendar

Math Objectives That Meet Standards

Children will:
1. Recognize, describe, extend, and creates a variety of patterns.
2. Use patterns to predict what comes next.

How to Do It

- The calendar offers a multitude of opportunities to look for patterns.
- Choose a pattern to do each week. With four- and five-year-olds, focus on the days-of-the-week patterns. With five- and six-year-olds, focus primarily on the numbers.
  - What comes after six in one, two, three, four, five, six, __?
  - What are some repeating patterns?
  - What comes after six in two, four, six, __?
  - What comes after seven in one, three, five, seven, __?
  - What comes after 15 in five, 10, 15, __?
  - What comes after 21 in one, three, six, 10, 15, 21, __?
  - What are some numerical patterns diagonally? Vertically?
  - What is the pattern of the days of the week we come to school?
  - What is the pattern of weeks in a month? Months in a year?

Patterns on a Geoboard

Materials

geoboards and rubber bands (see
"Geoboards" on page 91 of
Chapter 5)
cardstock
index cards
markers
scissors
glue
basket
laminating machine or clear contact
paper

Math Objectives That Meet Standards

Children will:
1. Replicate a pattern.
2. Recognize, describe, extend, and create a variety of patterns.

How to Do It

○ Let the children explore the geoboard and rubber bands to see how to use them.

○ Draw several shapes on index cards and challenge the children to duplicate those patterns on the geoboard. Start with basic shapes like circles and triangles, but as the children become more comfortable with the activity, set out more difficult shapes, such as stars. The rubber band designs can be superimposed one upon the next, moving from a simple square to polygons to other multisided irregular shapes.

○ Start by making multiple copies of basic designs and adding other designs to them. Use different colors to draw the rubber bands on the pattern cards so the children can "see through" through the layers of the design.

○ The rubber bands don't necessarily need to match but the different layers of color need to show on the cards.

○ Back the cards with cardstock and laminate them for a longer life.

○ Younger children may need a helping hand to show them what to do in this self-directed activity.

Take It Up a Level

Have the children design their own pattern cards and challenge each other to make each other's designs.

In Addition

In my experience, four- to five-year-olds use rubber bands responsibly. A little talk about safe use is useful. Redirect unacceptable behavior. The most prevalent undesirable use of rubber bands is chewing them. It doesn't seem to matter that they don't taste good. The best you are going to be able to do is reduce occurrences.

Block Pattern Cards

Math Objectives That Meet Standards

Children will:
1. Replicate a pattern.
2. Recognize, describe, extend, and create a variety of patterns.

Materials

butcher paper
scissors
markers and brown crayons
laminating machine or clear contact
    paper

How to Do It

- This pattern-matching activity is best when done in the Block Center. Because blocks activities are open-ended and because the children can put many of their own ideas into play, this activity is a big draw.
- Cut approximately fifteen 8" x 36" strips from the butcher paper, and use them to make block pattern cards.
- Trace the outlines of various block shapes on the cards. Create AB, ABC, and ABCD block patterns on them, as in the illustration below.
- Color the block silhouettes brown. Laminate them for longer life.
- Put the laminated block-pattern cards in the Block Center.
- The children select a pattern, find the blocks that match the block silhouettes, and put the blocks on top of the cards.
- After that, challenge the children to match the block patterns without placing the blocks on the pattern cards, or by placing the blocks beside the pattern cards.

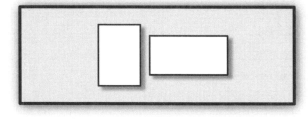 

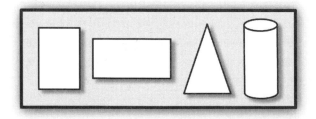 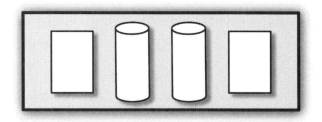

Take It Up a Level

Put the block-pattern cards on the chalk tray in a random sequence or pin them on the bulletin board. Ask the children to match the blocks they are playing with on the floor to patterns they see on the chalk tray or bulletin board.

Complete-the-Pattern Game

Materials

stickers
brown paper lunch bags
markers

Math Objectives That Meet Standards

Children will:

1. Use patterns to predict what comes next.
2. Replicate a pattern.
3. Identify the missing elements of a repeating pattern.

How to Do It

○ Place a bag down, flap side up, and attach stickers along its centerline in an AB pattern, from the open end of the bag to the upper edge of the bag flap.

○ Draw a question mark on the flap and put a box around it (see illustration below).

○ Make second and third bags with ABC and ABCD patterns on each, respectively.

○ Glue complete-the-game stickers on a fourth bag.

○ Cut out the stickers, leaving a brown paper border.

○ Lift the flap of the bag and attach the answer sticker under the bag flap.

○ The children use the stickers to extend the patterns that you started. They check their answers by looking under the bag flap.

○ Store the complete-the-pattern bag stickers in the bag.

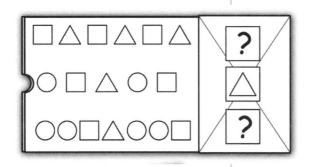

Take It Up a Level

Let the children make their own Complete-the-Pattern Games.

Playing Card Pattern Game

Materials

deck of playing cards
two math stands, each made from
   9" x 12" sheets of construction
   paper
scissors
glue
basket

Math Objectives That Meet Standards

Children will:
1. Use patterns to predict what comes next.
2. Identify missing elements of a repeating pattern.
3. Replicate a pattern.

How to Do It

- Follow the instructions on appendix page 164 that explain how to make the math stand. Because for this activity you will need a longer tray to work on, use 9" x 12" construction paper and make two of them.
- Use the playing cards to set up a pattern on the math stand. For example, set up the two of hearts, two of spades, and king of hearts (AAB).
- Have the children extend the pattern until they run out of space on the math stands.
- Do a couple of patterns during Group Time and then move the activity to the Math or Games and Puzzles Center.
- Put the playing cards in the basket next to the trays so the children can work independently to form patterns.
- Encourage children to invite a friend to play simple pattern-extension games with the cards.

Take It Up a Level

Encourage the children to draw the playing card patterns on paper.

Photograph Patterns

Materials

clothesline
basket
clothespins
photographs of all of the children
   (see "Photo Graph" on page 108)

Math Objectives That Meet Standards

Children will:
1. Recognize patterns in the physical world.
2. Recognize, describe, extend, and create a variety of patterns.

How to Do It

- Set up a clothesline similar to the one in the illustration on page 30.
- Clip the pictures of the children to the clothesline in a simple pattern.
- Do not put up the last photo in the pattern you are using.
- Let the children have time to examine the pattern and mull over the best picture to use to complete the pattern.
- Repeat AB, AAB, ABB patterns several times until the children understand the idea. When they do, let the children work independently and challenge friends to complete, copy, or extend patterns they have made.

- Here are some photograph patterns to use:
  - Boy, girl, boy, girl, _____
  - Long hair, short hair, long hair, _____
  - Long-sleeve shirt, short-sleeve shirt, long-sleeve shirt, _____
  - Brown eyes, blue eyes, brown eyes, _____

Take It Up a Level

Have the children draw themselves and then use the drawings to create and extend patterns.

In Addition

A clotheslines made from pony tail yarn can add interest to a classroom. Put it across a corner of the room at the children's sitting height (sitting on the floor). Attach photographs with clothespins for the children to make patterns. It will be an irresistible activity, so you will need a waiting list on a clipboard to be sure everyone gets a turn to make patterns with photographs.

Patterns with Buttons

Materials

buttons from "Button Graph" on page 106
sentence strip
container
marker

Math Objectives That Meet Standards

Children will:
1. Use patterns to predict what comes next.
2. Sort and classify concrete objects by one or more attributes.
3. Seriate objects.

How to Do It

- Draw 1" diameter circles ½" apart on a sentence strip, as shown in the illustration below.
- The sentence strip base keeps the activity organized.
- Demonstrate how to make simple patterns in the circles on sentence strip, such as AB, AAB, ABC, and ABAB, ABCABC.
- Continue to the end of the sentence strip.
- Let the children help you decide which button pattern to create.
- This is an open-ended activity where almost any pattern is acceptable if they can explain the pattern.
- Set this activity up in the Math Center for independent work.

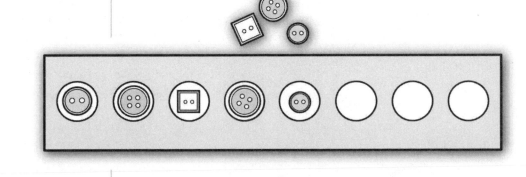

Patterns with Pompoms

Materials

three large pompoms per child doing
    the activity
three small Styrofoam trays with
    small amounts of different colors
    of tempera paint in each tray for
    each child doing the activity
newspaper to cover work area
paper towels for urgent cleanup
three clothespins for each child
    doing the activity
9" x 12" sheets of paper
basket

Count on This

Easel paper, brushes, and containers
of tempera paint are tools for
creativity. The children start, and
they end, but the fun is in the
middle.

Math Objectives That Meet Standards

Children will:
1. Recognize, describe, extend, and create a variety of patterns.

How to Do It

- Introduce this activity during Group Time, and demonstrate doing
  several patterns so the children understand what to do. This is a
  wonderful activity to move to the Art Center once the children
  know how to do it.
- This activity is potentially messy, but there are several things to
  do to keep the mess to a minimum.
- Cover a workspace with newspaper and put out the small trays of
  tempera paint along the top of the workspace.
- Put the pompoms and the clothespins in the basket.
- Give each child a piece of paper and challenge all of them to use
  the clothespins to pick up a pompom and dip it into the paint to
  make a print.
- After printing, have the children return the clothespin with the
  pompom still attached to the tray of paint so they can be used
  again with a minimum of mess.
- Encourage the children to dip alternate pompoms in different
  colors or paint to make a row of patterns (see illustration below).

"Cup Tapping" Patterns

Math Objectives That Meet Standards

Children will:
1. Recognize, describe, extend, and create a variety of patterns.
2. Replicate a pattern.

Materials

two paper or plastic cups
    (3- or 4-ounce) for each child
chart and stand
marker

How to Do It

- Set up this activity in the Library Center so children can work independently after you explain it to the group.
- With the children, sing the song below, or recite it as a poem.
- Encourage the children to learn the words to "Cup Tapping," and after they know them, write the words on a chart.
- Demonstrate the actions for each line to the children.
- Give each child two cups.
- Have the chart and the drawings visible to all the children so they can tap along with the song, using the drawings as their guide.
- After the children are familiar with the patterns, put away the chart and ask them to make their own tapping patterns.

Cup Tapping by Sharon MacDonald
(from *the Watermelon Pie and Other Tunes!* CD by Sharon MacDonald)

These cups (tap bottoms of cups together horizontally)
Are made for tapping, (tap mouths of cups together horizontally)
It's a funny (tap bottoms of cups together horizontally)
Little game I play. (tap mouths of cups horizontally)

I tap them here. (tap bottoms of cups horizontally)
I tap them there. (tap mouths of cups horizontally)
Come play (tap mouths of cups horizontally)
My funny game this way. (tap bottoms of cups horizontally)

Tap in and out, (tap cup lips so one is inside the other)
And in and out. (tap cup sides together vertically)
Tap down, and down, and down. (tap cup mouths on ground)

Tap over, (tap cup mouths together vertically)
Under, (tap cup bottoms together vertically)
On your head. (tap cup mouths on sides of head)

Tap all your body 'round. (tap cups along body)

What Is ...?

Symmetry means balance to the mind and to the eye. It is a central organizing idea that guides how we do things and it suggests completeness. It is also a pattern. Our need for symmetry asks that things be in proportion in size, shape, and position. Most things we find beautiful arise from our intuitive sense of symmetry. Symmetry is important to math because it invites order, balance, proportion, and completeness.

Symmetry and Blocks

Materials

blocks
36" strip of colored tape

What Is ...?

There is **rotation symmetry**— rotation around an axis—in a tricycle wheel that spins. In the classroom, rotational symmetry is reproduced when parquetry blocks are rotated around an axis through the center of a parquetry-block pattern.

Math Objectives That Meet Standards

Children will:

1. Identify the missing elements in a repeating pattern.
2. Demonstrate an awareness of symmetry.
3. Replicate a pattern.

How to Do It

- This is a small-group activity for the Block Center. Demonstrate the activity in Group Time or in groups of three or four children as they come into the Block Center.
- Have two children sit in two chairs, facing each other. Place a 36" tape strip on the floor between the two children. Give each child five or six blocks.
- One child leads the other. The leader puts down a block on her side of the tape, and the child opposite puts his block in the same position, opposite the first block.
- Encourage the leader to put the first block at the tape line and work outward with all blocks touching. This way, the symmetry is clearer. The leader can get fancy later!
- When all of the blocks have been placed, the children stand over the block structure to see the symmetry. After all the blocks are laid out, have the children switch roles and continue.

Symmetry and Mylar Mirrors

Materials

folding, two-panel mirror made from Mylar
single mirror made from Mylar
cardboard
masking or strapping tape
objects to reflect
apple sheet (see illustration on appendix page 179)
index cards
large index card or cardstock
markers
basket

Math Objectives That Meet Standards

Children will:

1. Identify the missing elements in a repeating pattern.
2. Demonstrate an awareness of symmetry.
3. Replicate a pattern.

How to Do It

- Glue small sheets of Mylar, slightly smaller than 4" x 6" to three pieces of cardboard to make two small mirrors.
- Attach tape around the edges to secure the Mylar mirrors to the cardboard. Tape the two Mylar mirrors together, leaving about ¼" gap between them, so the mirrors will fold easily.
- Copy the two apple halves in the illustration on appendix page 179 onto index cards.
- On a large index card or piece of cardstock, create a picture direction card (also called a task card), which is a pictorial representation of the steps of the activity. This enables the children to do the activity independently.
- Demonstrate in Group Time how to use the mirrors to reflect concrete and pictorial objects, and to explore part/whole relationships.
- Put the apple pattern cards, a picture direction card, and the Mylar mirrors in a basket in the Math Center for the children to explore making whole objects out of halves.
- Use other objects, pictures, and drawings as needed to keep interest up and to continue to explore symmetry.

String Painting Symmetry

Math Objectives That Meet Standards

Children will:

1. Demonstrate an awareness of symmetry.
2. Represent commonly used fractions (⅛, ¼, ⅓, ½).

Materials

four 12" lengths of cotton string
four 4" x 8" washed Styrofoam meat trays with different colors of tempera paint in each
four 6" x 12" washed Styrofoam meat trays to contain the paint trays
masking tape
newspaper
paper towels
white construction paper (9" x 12")

How to Do It

- Demonstrate the activity during Group Time, then set it up in the Art Center for independent work.
- Cover the work area with newspaper.
- Tape loops in each piece of string with masking tape to make a handles for the children to hold to remove the strings from the paint.
- Put the smaller Styrofoam trays with paint on the larger trays.
- Put one string in each of the four paint trays. Let the handle hang over the tray edge.
- To do the activity, have a child pick up a sheet of white paper, fold the paper in half, and unfold it.
- Have the child remove a string from the color tray and place it on one side of the paper, fold the paper over the string with the handle sticking out from the top, and press the paper against the string to make an imprint.
- Ask the child to open the paper, remove the string by the handle, and place the string back in the tray so the handle hangs over the edge of the paint tray, ready for the next child.
- Put the symmetrical imprints aside to dry and then display them for all the children to see the different designs.

Symmetry Puzzle

Materials

three sheets of different-colored
    cardstock
scissors
marker
glue
laminating machine or clear contact
    paper

Math Objectives That Meet Standards

Children will:

1. Demonstrate an awareness of symmetry.
2. Represent commonly used fractions (⅛, ¼, ⅓, ½).

How to Do It

- Place two sheets of cardstock on top of one another.
- Draw a design, starting and returning to the left edge of the cardstock sheets.
- Cut out the design.
- Separate the sheets and glue them to a third sheet in a symmetrical design (see illustration on appendix page 180).
- Cut the construction into puzzle pieces, into as many pieces as you think will challenge the children.
- Laminate the pieces for durability.
- Put the activity in the Games and Puzzles Center for individual exploration.

Reflections on Symmetry

Materials

Reflections by Ann Jonas

Math Objectives That Meet Standards

Children will:

1. Identify the missing elements of a repeating pattern.
2. Demonstrate an awareness of symmetry.
3. Represent commonly used fractions (⅛, ¼, ⅓, ½).

How to Do It

- *Reflections* is a must-have for the early childhood classroom. Use it at Story Time. Little introduction is required—just show the book cover and start turning the pages: fishermen, the lighthouse, the ferry, sailboats, and birds. It goes through the day and seemingly ends in the forest.
- Then, turn the book over. The book goes back through the same pictures with a revised storyline.
- Starting over upside down always brings an "Oh!" from the children.
- Have *Reflections* available in the Library Center for exploration after you have read it during Group Time. It will be a popular book.

Take It Up a Level

Challenge the children to draw a reflection.

Problem Solving and Reasoning

CHAPTER 8

What Is ...?

Problem solving means finding solutions and posing questions. Young children come to problem solving easily because they are naturally curious and enthusiastic about new experiences. Their curiosity leads them to explore different objects' qualities and characteristics, some of which are measurable. Early childhood is a great time to help children start assembling the tools they need to figure out the world. Not surprisingly, young children do not immediately acquire problem-solving skills. It takes time for skills to develop, and because children enter school with various levels of math understanding, assessment is a challenge.

The most important thing a teacher can do to teach problem-solving and reasoning skills is to use as teaching opportunities the normal situations that occur in the classroom everyday. These situations are not contrived—they happen all the time.

The activities in this chapter will take you through classroom events that actually happened. These activities seek to answer the question, "How can I let the children find solutions to more of the problems and frustrations they confront in their everyday interactions with their peers?" by providing the framework for problem solving rather than solutions themselves.

How do children solve problems? They use reasoning skills, just like adults.

What Is ...?

Reasoning means thinking, explaining one's thoughts and coming up with a plan. Reasoning is a systematic, flexible approach. It is a learned behavior.

Children reason from their own experiences and trust their reasoning skills to guide them to their own unique solutions in a variety of situations. Many of their thought-based accomplishments go unheralded because, often, adults do not give them credit for the abilities they have. Children do have unique ways to solve problems that develop from their individual points of view.

In early childhood classrooms, we can instill in the children an inclination toward flexibility, observation, and creating systematic approaches to problem solving. The classic Aesop's fable, "The Crow and the Pitcher," presents a wonderful example of real-world problem solving—observation and thought before action. Read it with your children.

Aesop's fables are wonderful for storytelling—they teach lessons by embedding them in everyday experience. Learning flows from experience, and it is especially important that young children learn in a similar way as the crow in Aesop's fable.

The Problem-Solving Process

Here is a real-life problem-solving exercise with apples.

A jar full of red apples is a momentary curiosity in a young child's day. One day, however, I passed a jar of apples around the class, and asked the children, "How many apples are in the jar?" Each child guessed a number. Group Time ended before all of the children could guess a number and they were on their way to centers before I got an answer to how many apples were in the jar.

Following up, I asked four of the children to be our "research" team to find out how many apples were in the jar (while the rest of the children were busy in centers). They agreed. I gave each team member an index card and a pencil to write answers. I asked them to report to the class after their research was completed. I observed and made mental notes of the process.

They tried to count the apples in the closed jar. There was a discussion. The answers they got were: three, 16, 50, and 39. Quite a difference! One child suggested taking off the lid and counting them. They did. Apples rolled everywhere. The children walked to each fallen apple and counted it where it sat and recounted the total number of apples again. Once again, there were big differences in answers.

Another child suggested putting all the apples together. They did. Soon, they had a group of apples. They circled and counted: 120 apples. "Too many," they said, "the pile was not that big." Finally, one of the children started lining up apples in a row. The rest joined in. They counted and agreed: 12. They were thrilled. But, how do you write "12?" No one knew for sure. One of the children decided to go over to the Science Center to get a number line. He put it down and put the apples on it. There it was, "12," right there on the number line. There was a sigh of relief and a small celebration as they all wrote "12" on their index cards.

They paced impatiently, like pint-size professors, as they waited to report to the rest of the class. Proudly, they displayed the "12" on each of their index cards as they reported their findings: "12 apples in the

The Problem-Solving Process

1. State the question or problem.
2. Propose a solution.
3. Revise the first solution.
4. Revise the solution again.
5. State a new, related problem.
6. Propose a new solution

jar!" All of the earlier estimates were checked against the actual count by the research team. After they shared their answers, the research team described how they found the answer. From then on, most of the children in class knew "12" and could count objects on the number line. And what about the number line? It took on new meaning to all the children: it became a tool.

This story relates how the problem-solving methods embedded in what the children are already doing serve as powerful and enjoyable learning opportunities. The research team went through an orderly and logical process that led to a solution. The process was:

- ◎ **State the question or problem**: How many apples in the jar?
- ◎ **Propose a solution**: Count the apples in the jar.
- ◎ **Revised solution #1**: Count them scattered on the floor.
- ◎ **Revised solution #2**: Count them in a row.
- ◎ **State a new, related problem**: How do you write "12"?
- ◎ **Propose a new solution**: Put apples on a number line and count them, and use the last number, "12."

We want children to solve problems using a structured process similar to the one above: to decide what it is they want to know, and then to suggest their own solution steps based on their own assessment of what information they need.

The teacher helps by giving the children a nudge in the right direction when they get off track, and by offering suggestions when they are stumped. It is important, however, that the children have freedom to "work" the problems out themselves. After using the steps, and revising them if results prove inaccurate, we want them to check results to see how they did.

In early education, the **process** children use to solve problems is more important than the answers they get.

Young children need hundreds of experiences solving problems to become good problem solvers. Over time, problems become more complicated. Problems solved mathematically may initially require that the children count. Later on, they will be required to add and to use multiple steps using any number of mathematical tools. A good problem solver poses the right questions, organizes the information they have gathered, makes reasonable estimates, checks work, draws conclusions, and makes predictions about future situations that are similar to the problem they are working at the moment.

The activities that follow are examples of problems embedded in the children's everyday activities and experiences that offer problem-solving opportunities using a structured process, similar to the apple activity discussed above. You can set up similar situations to answer different questions, depending on what your class wants to know.

Activities That Teach Problem Solving and Reasoning

The Little Plant That Could

Materials

plants to grow from a seedling
water
window with outdoor light
ruler
chart paper and marker

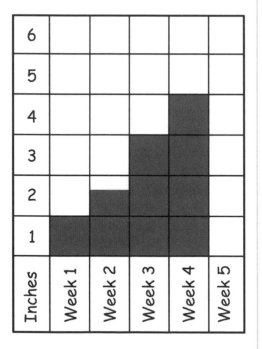

Math Objectives That Meet Standards

Children will:
1. State the problem or question.
2. Make a step-by-step plan to solve a problem.
3. Follow a data-collection plan.
4. Organize information to solve problems and answer questions.

Background and Children's Solution

We were studying a science unit, in which the children planted seeds and watched plants grow over time. One child, Jason, was convinced his plant was not growing like the other children's plants. He wanted to see big changes in the plant's size, right away. The children and I proposed the question, "How can we tell if Jason's plant is growing?" The children generated some ideas about how to answer the question.

As they brainstormed, I wrote their ideas on a chart. The children suggested:

- Use a ruler to measure the plant every day.
- Keep a time line to show how much it is growing.

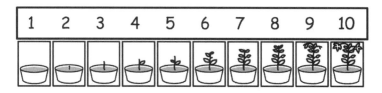

- Photograph the plant every Friday.
- Count on your fingers to see how tall it is.

We voted and combined solutions. The measuring with a ruler won, but we measured once a week (see the illustration on the next page).

Each Friday we filled in a column on the graph showing the growth of the plant (see the illustration on the left). Jason was relieved to see that his plant actually was growing and that maybe, someday, it would catch up to the rest. Interestingly, he stopped noticing that some other children's plants were bigger. He was just fine with his. We called it "the little plant that could."

If you are interested in having a similar experience in the classroom, or a situation like this naturally occurs,

○ Bring in plants for the children to watch grow, or give them seeds to plant themselves.

○ When the children express interest in knowing how much their plants are growing, or if they are growing at all, let them come up with ways to measure thge growth, such as putting a ruler in the plant's pot, as shown in the illustration on the left.

○ To keep track of the growth in an organized fashion, create a graph, like the one shown on the previous page.

○ Every Friday, help the children record the increases in their plants' sizes on the graph.

How Many for Lunch?

Materials

Yes-and-No Graph Bag (see page 111)
cardstock
scissors

Math Objectives That Meet Standards

Children will:
1. Decide if there is enough information to solve the problem.
2. Select and use appropriate mathematical tools.
3. Follow a plan for collecting information.
4. Select and apply a problem-solving strategy.

Background and Children's Solution

Each morning at our school, the cafeteria staff needed to have classes report by 10:00 the number of children who would be having school lunch. Turning that task over the children seemed like a good idea since it would free up my time and offer an opportunity for the children to learn problem-solving skills. During Group Time, I asked the children if they could think of another way to get the lunch count without my asking each of them every day.

We stated the problem, "Who is having school lunch?" and I wrote it on a narrow cardstock strip. We started talking about how to do it. Here were some suggestions:

○ Sign our names on a piece of paper on the door.
○ Use our Yes-and-No Graph Bag.
○ Have the class leader for the day get a clipboard and put a mark beside each child's name.
○ Use our Jug Tallys.

The *Yes-and-No Graph Bag* was the winner. To use it for this purpose, I put Velcro on the back of a strip of cardstock with our question, "Who is having lunch?" written on it, and put the card at the top of the bag. Each day next to the bag, I laid out cards with the children's names on them. As they came through the door in the morning, the children put their names in either the *yes* or *no* column. The class leader for the day counted the yeses, wrote the number on an index card and took it to the cafeteria. Afterward, I removed the "who is having lunch" tag so we could use the graph bag for other activities.

If you are interested in having a similar experience in the classroom, or a situation like this naturally occurs,

- Challenge the children to come up with ways to determine what number to send to the cafeteria staff.
- Help the children determine what the most effective method would be (likely something similar to the above solution), and help them implement it.
- Select one child to be the class leader, and help that child collect the number and deliver it to the cafeteria.

How Do You Make a Jelly Sandwich with One Slice of Bread?

Materials

1-ounce cups, one for each child
jelly (to put in the 1-ounce cups (vote for the selections to be used)
slice of bread (one per child)
plastic knife (one per child)
small paper plate (one per child)
tray for the cups of jelly

Math Objectives That Meet Standards

Children will:
1. Define the problem and state the question.
2. Make a step-by-step plan to solve a problem.
3. Follow a plan.
4. Explain the reasonableness of a solution.
5. Represent commonly used fractions ($\frac{1}{8}$, $\frac{1}{4}$, $\frac{1}{3}$, $\frac{1}{2}$).
6. Understand part/whole relationships.

Background and Children's Solution

The children were learning about parts, wholes, and the one-half fraction ($\frac{1}{2}$). They were having difficulty understanding that two halves make a whole. I devised this activity to help their understanding. Before the children arrived for school, I put cups of jelly on a tray, some plastic knives in a tall plastic cup, and a slice of bread on each of the children's paper plates. I stacked the paper plates with bread close to the worktable.

During Group Time, we talked about sandwiches and the parts of a sandwich, (top, middle, and bottom). We discussed the origins of the sandwich (see In Addition on the following page). Because we had only one slice of bread for each child, I explained, the children would have to make their sandwiches with just one slice. We had our question: How can we make a sandwich with one slice of bread?

The children went to the worktable during center time, got their plates with their single slices of bread, wrote their names on their plates, and each got one cup of jelly and a plastic knife. Some of the children cut their bread in half with the knife while some tore the bread in half. Others folded. We discovered that it took approximately equal halves of bread to make a sandwich. They learned more about the fraction one-half ($\frac{1}{2}$) and part/whole relationships. Eventually, each child made a sandwich, tossed out the jelly cup and knife and put the sandwiches on their plates. We would all have our snack together.

Each child came up with a plan and implemented it. After snack time, we talked about how we made the sandwiches. Some of the children drew the steps they took to make the sandwich. Others were able to describe the process aloud.

In Addition

The name sandwich comes from the Fourth Earl of Sandwich, an English nobleman (1718–1792). He liked to play table games (actually he was an insatiable gambler, but the children probably don't need to know that). He did not want to stop playing games to eat, so he demanded his food be served between two slices of bread. He could eat with one hand and play with the other! I explained to the children that half of the Earl's body wanted to play games while the other half wanted to eat. They related to that.

If you are interested in having a similar experience in the classroom, or a situation like this naturally occurs,

- During Group Time, talk to the children about the different parts of a jelly sandwich and the history of the sandwich, and ask the children how they might make a sandwich with just one slice of bread.
- Give each child a paper plate, help to write the children's names on their plates, set out the jelly and the plastic knives, and challenge them to make a sandwich with one slice of bread.
- After the children finish making and enjoying their sandwiches, ask them to describe the different ways they went about making the sandwiches.
- Encourage the children to make drawings of the steps, if they wish.

Where Is Sarah?

Materials

classroom and children (Sarah could be any child in the classroom)

Math Objectives That Meet Standards

Children will:

1. Identify alternative ways to solve verbal and written problems.
2. Decide if there is enough information to solve the problem.
3. Define the problem and state the question.

Background and Children's Solution

Note: This activity is similar to "Obstacle Course," found in Chapter 5, but here poses itself as a problem to solve in this activity.

One day, when the children were busy during Center Time, I stopped the class to ask, "Where is Sarah?" (meaning her physical location in the classroom).

When the children located her in the room, I encouraged them to describe how to find her. Some of the suggestions were:

- Measure with a tape measure.
- Count the floor tiles across the floor to Sarah.
- Walk to Sarah and count the steps.
- Everyone hold hands until they reach Sarah.
- Talk about the furniture and equipment near Sarah.

Counting the floor tiles won. I started walking off the tiles from one side of the room toward the center, but I was not close to Sarah. The children were baffled. We discussed the way that we could start from anywhere in the classroom, but that counting in a straight line along the tiles wouldn't necessarily bring us to Sarah. Also, simply saying that Sarah was a certain number of tiles from the wall wouldn't let other children know where in the room Sarah stood, either. What to do? We decided that we had to count across the room, then over/up/down to Sarah.

The class leader for the day wrote on a clipboard, for instance, "10 across and 7 over" to Sarah. I drew a grid-like map of our classroom floor, so the children could chart the steps and see what they had done. We talked about how our first plan had to change, and how we made a new plan. From then on the children found everything in the classroom by counting the number of floor tiles: across and then up/over/down. They took to playing games with one another, challenging each other to locate different objects in the room. Lots of fun!

If you are interested in having a similar experience in the classroom, or a situation like this naturally occurs,

- Point to a certain child or object in the room, and challenge the children to think of ways to map her location.
- After the children find a way to indicate where in the classroom the child or object is located, help the children recreate their method of locating the child or object on paper.

How Many Swings Make One Turn?

Materials

playground swings
timer (one that ticks and then "dings" when it stops)

Math Objectives That Meet Standards

Children will:
1. Explore and solve simple problems.
2. Define the problem and state the question.
3. Make a step-by-step plan to solve a problem.
4. Look for patterns to predict solutions.

Background and Children's Solution

Playground swings are in short supply in most schools, yet most children want to swing. Often, this leads to congestion at the swing sets during outside play. The best way to assure that every child who wants to swing gets to do it is to take turns. But how do you do it? No child wants to be second or third on a take-turns list because turns take a long time.

At Group Time, I talked with the children about how long a turn on a swing should be, since young children are still developing a concept of time: if they are waiting, a minute can seem like forever; if they are playing, a minute can pass like a snap of the fingers. All the children agreed that a turn should be longer than a minute "if you are having fun."

I asked if they could think about how many swings made a turn. I wrote our problem on a chart: "How many swings make a turn?" I wanted the children to think about the problem overnight, and told them would discuss it at Group Time the following day.

The next day, we brought up the question: How many swings make a turn? The children offered several solutions:

- Ask the principal (he or she will know).
- Push the swing, watch and count.
- Put someone in the swing, push and count for one turn.
- Put someone in the swing and push it so the swing won't be so high (children who swing high take longer than those who don't).
- Use the kitchen timer to count the swings.

We discussed how we would probably have to put several of the plans together to answer our question, and came up with this solution: a child would sit in the swing, and another child would push so the swing would go upward the same distance. One child set and watched the timer and the swings, another tallied, and all of the rest of the children would count the upswings, out loud.

It was a wonderful experience. The children were completely in the moment, totally focused on the task. When they realized there were plenty of swings in a minute, they decided that a minute was lots of time.

For several weeks, the children took the timer outside to time the swings. Later they just counted. It was close enough, they thought. Still later, they "just knew" how long a minute was, and got off the swing to give the next child a turn. Getting the children involved worked. Problem solved!

By the way, there are about 30 swings per minute. Your "mileage" may vary.

If you are interested in having a similar experience in the classroom, or a situation like this naturally occurs,

- Ask the children how long they think one child's ride on a swing should last. Encourage them to go home and think about the answer overnight.
- If a child does not suggest timing, make the suggestion, or take out the stopwatch and ask the children how they could use it to determine how long a ride on the swings should last.
- After the children determine what an appropriate length for a ride on the swings will be, tell them they will get to test their suggestion.
- When the children go outside, bring the timer with them, and encourage them to work together, selecting one child at a time to be the timekeeper, one to swing, and one to push the person on the swing.

How Many Cans and Boxes?

Materials

Home Center (or a grocery store area in the classroom)

shelving

variety of small boxes and cans (to simulate grocery-store shelves)

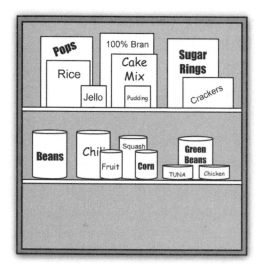

Count on This

After doing this activity, the children in my classroom made a game out of box and can cleanup in the Home Center. The pots and pans, on the other hand, were another story.

Math Objectives That Meet Standards

Children will:

1. Explore and solve simple, vocalized problems.
2. Find and describe the question in the problem.
3. Make a step-by-step plan to solve a problem.
4. Look at patterns to predict solutions.
5. Select and apply a strategy to solve a problem.

Background and Children's Solution

Parents brought in empty cereal, cake, rice, and cracker boxes and empty cans of various sizes with the labels still attached. I put the boxes and cans in a clothesbasket and set the basket in the Home Center. To begin, I explained that the boxes and cans needed to be put away on the shelves in the Home Center so everything was visible, and easy to put away. When the children gathered in the Home Center, I gave each child one or two cans or boxes. I let the children describe ways to organize the shelves. Their suggestions were:

- Put the boxes on one shelf and all the cans on another.
- Put the boxes in the back and the cans in the front.
- Put the boxes on the bottom shelves and the cans on the top shelves.
- Put all the boxes on one shelf with the tallest ones on the back and the shorter ones up front; do the same with the cans.

We voted. "Tallest ones on the back" won. We put all the tall cereal boxes together, and then compared the other sizes of boxes (cake, rice, and cracker boxes) until we had four different sizes of boxes seriated on the shelf (see illustration below). We followed the same procedure with the cans. When the children looked at the shelves, they could see all of the boxes and cans on the shelves because we used height as the criteria for organizing them.

If you are interested in having a similar experience in the classroom, or a situation like this naturally occurs,

- Send home a note asking parents to bring in empty cereal, cake, rice, and cracker boxes and empty cans of various sizes.
- Challenge the children to find a way to organize the boxes and cans on the shelves so that everything is visible.
- Once the children offer up several ideas, vote on them or choose to combine several good ideas, and set out implementing them.
- When the children are done, have them look at the shelves. They should be able to see all of the boxes and cans because of the way they are organized.

What's Near, What's Far?

Materials

hallway leading to various places like the bathroom, cafeteria, and library

Math Objectives That Meet Standards

Children will:
1. Select and apply a strategy to solve a problem.
2. Explore and solve a simple, verbalized problem.
3. Find and describe the question in the problem.
4. Make a step-by-step plan to solve a problem.

Background and Children's Solution

During one school year, a child, Michael, broke his leg and he was fitted with a walking cast. The doctor warned that Michael could only walk short distances. He would have to ride in a wheelchair if he needed to go any long distances. Michael reported the doctor's walking and riding conditions to the rest of the children when he returned to school in his shiny new cast, and in a wheelchair pushed by his mother.

The children had no idea how far short and long distances were, but we wanted to make a list for Michael so everyone would know what to do and how to help. Most of the places Michael could walk to were simple to decide. He could walk anywhere in the classroom. He could walk to the bathroom. These places were close. The library was a little farther away, but was it a long distance? The cafeteria was far, everyone agreed, but how far? We posed the questions: What is a short distance, what is a long distance, and what can we do to find out?

The children proposed these plans to find out:
- Measure the distance with a tape measure;
- Ask the custodian;
- Walk to a far place and count the steps; and
- See how many steps it is to the bathroom, and then to the cafeteria, and then how many more to the library. Add everything.

We chose the last plan of action, "how many steps." We selected two children to walk off the number of steps to the bathroom. Once they determined the distance, they reported their findings to the children. Together, everyone walked to the cafeteria, because the children couldn't count all the steps required to go that far. After we got back to the classroom, I reported the distance in steps to everyone. Finally, we had a set of totals from which to work: 31 steps to the bathroom, 85 steps to the cafeteria, and 40 steps to the library.

From the information the children gathered, we could make a list for Michael of all the places to which he could walk. He could walk around the classroom and to the bathroom and the library, but he would have to ride in his wheelchair to the cafeteria. All the children volunteered to push the wheelchair. How we managed that was another problem for them to solve.

If you are interested in having a similar experience in the classroom, or a situation like this naturally occurs,

○ Ask the children what they think constitutes a "close" distance, and what constitutes a "far" distance. Consider using the examples from above: is the front of the room near or far, is the bathroom near or far? Are the library and the cafeteria near or far? Use other locations in your school that you think make sense.

○ Ask the children to think of ways to determine what distances are near and far.

○ Challenge the children to experiment with the best examples they suggest, and record the results.

○ From the information the children gather, make a list for of all the places that are near and far.

How Many Days Until Thanksgiving?

Materials

calendar

Count on This

To relieve anxiety revealed by the children's repeated "When's the party?" questions, give them something visual to count or mark off. They will be much less anxious and you will have to answer fewer questions.

Math Objectives That Meet Standards

Children will:
1. Select and use appropriate mathematical tools.
2. Explain the reasonableness of solutions.
3. Select and apply strategies to solve a problem.
4. Decide if enough information is present to a solve problem.

Background and Children's Solution

Our kindergarten classes were going to have a Thanksgiving feast and each class was responsible for bringing one of the food dishes. The children were excited about our get-together and they asked every day—and I mean every day—"When are we going to have our Thanksgiving feast?"

I decided I had heard the question enough. I pulled the children together on their carpet squares and I pointed to our class calendar. "What day are we going to celebrate Thanksgiving?" I asked. The children found the turkey I had drawn on the calendar and noted that the date was Thursday, November 25. We talked about our feast being one day before Thanksgiving. "What day was that?" I asked. They answered. I asked the children how they could count the number of days remaining before our Thanksgiving feast.

The plan: Count the number of days on the calendar separating that day and the day with the turkey drawn on it.

This was the only suggestion the children made. We started counting on November 11. There were 14 days until Thanksgiving, so 13 days until our feast. At the end of each day, the children wanted to mark it off the calendar, then recount the days to see how many were left. It was a good suggestion, so at the end of each day, the day's class leader marked the calendar, and we counted the new number of days before Thanksgiving.

If you are interested in having a similar experience in the classroom, or a situation like this naturally occurs,

○ Pick a special upcoming date, and challenge the children to find ways of knowing how many days remain before that date arrives.

○ Set up a calendar and help the children organize a way of marking off the days.

In Addition

The following are additional questions the children can use to problem solve:

- ○ How many people are not here today?
- ○ What number does not belong?
- ○ How fast does ice melt?
- ○ Which puzzle piece will fit in this space?
- ○ How can you make the room look larger?
- ○ What other numbers will work?
- ○ How big will the gerbil grow? How can we find out?
- ○ What size cups do we need for the juice? Why?
- ○ Which objects are bigger? How do you know?
- ○ How hot is it beside the window?
- ○ How tall is the tree? How can we find out? Can we find out exactly?
- ○ How many apples do we need if everyone is going to eat half (½) of an apple?
- ○ How many weeks until next month?
- ○ How can we discover what color birds like best?
- ○ Which pumpkin weighs the most? Least? The same?
- ○ How long before we go to music?
- ○ How many playing cards can you toss in the hat?

Putting It All Together: A Pizza Unit Study

This chapter puts all the math skills together in a pizza-exclusive unit of study. Pizza is a food that many young children enjoy as part of their everyday world, so learning math through pizza is fun and meaningful for them. The children get pizza and ingest the math skills as a "side order," so to speak. It is much like the following humorous story of how hamburgers were "invented."

Hamburgers were invented to get children to eat salad—you know, lettuce, tomatoes, pickles. Most children don't like salad, even in Germany. Well, a wise mother put salad ingredients between two buns with a meat patty and, voilà: she had a salad disguised as a burger. She called it the salad burger. Well, when no child wanted a salad burger, she renamed it the hamburger, after the German city of Hamburg, where this wise mother lived. The hamburger idea spread all over the world. Children ate the meat and bread they loved in the hamburgers, and they also ate the healthy stuff, the salad, on the sly.

If you don't believe the story, that's OK. It's better with math and pizza anyway!

The activities that follow explain the skills and objectives they address as well as where in the previous chapters you can find them. The specific math skill you want to teach will depend upon your emphasis.

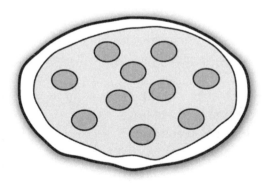

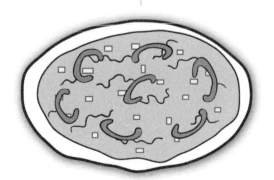

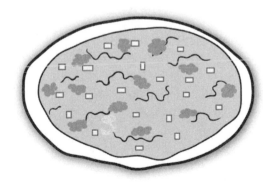

"Five Round Pizzas"

Materials

chef's hat

pizza pan

paper pizzas with a magnetic strip on the back (See illustration on appendix page 181)

paper dollars with a magnetic strip on the back (See illustration on appendix page 181)

Five Round Pizzas

by Sharon MacDonald

(Tune: "Five Little Honey Buns")

Five round pizzas in the pizza shop,
Big and round with melted cheese on
the top.
Along came (child's name) *with a*
dollar one day.
She (He) *bought a pizza pie and took*
it on his way.

Four round pizzas in the pizza shop,
(repeat the last three lines in the
first stanza)

Three round pizzas in the pizza shop,
(repeat the last three lines in the
first stanza)

Two round pizzas in the pizza shop,
(repeat the last three lines in the
first stanza)

One round pizza in the pizza shop,
(repeat the last three lines in the
first stanza)

No round pizzas in the pizza shop,
Big and round with melted cheese on
the top.
Along came (child's name) *with a*
dollar one day.
No pizza pie for her (him) *today.*

Math Objectives That Meet Standards

Children will:

1. Learn one-to-one correspondence (Chapter 2, Number Sense and Numeration).
2. Add and subtract whole numbers (Chapter 3, Computation and Estimation).
3. Explore the use and meaning of currency and coins (Chapter 4, Measurement, Time, and Money).
4. Describe and compare real-life objects to solid shapes (Chapter 5, Geometry and Spatial Sense).
5. Collect and organize data about themselves, their surroundings, and their meaningful experiences (Chapter 6, Sorting, Classifying, Graphing, Data Analysis, and Probability).
6. Use patterns to predict what comes next (Chapter 7, Patterns and Number Relationships).
7. Explore and solve simple, verbally stated problems (Chapter 8, Problem Solving and Reasoning).

How to Do It

- This is a great Group Time activity.
- Sing the "Five Round Pizzas" song with the children, encouraging them to act out the roles mentioned in the song, such as buying pizzas from the pizza chef.
- Using the pizza and dollar illustrations on appendix page 181, make five paper pizzas and six dollar bills available for the children to use to dramatize the story. They are easy enough to make.
- Put all the pizzas on the tray and give six children a cutout dollar bill. Give a seventh child the chef's hat, and have that child sit in a chair with the tray of pizzas to be the pizza chef. This child will receive the money.
- As the children sing the song, each child with $1.00 comes up to the pizza chef, takes a pizza from the tray, and leaves $1.00.
- When the last child comes with his $1.00 and finds there are no more pizzas, challenge all the children to decide what to do. (Usually, they decide that the child with the dollar gets to be the pizza chef and sells the pizzas in the next round.)
- All of the children in the class participate in turn; when they are not dramatizing the story, encourage them to sing the song.

Pizza Crusts

Materials

newspaper and magazine picture ads of pizza with different crusts
glue stick
sheet of chart paper

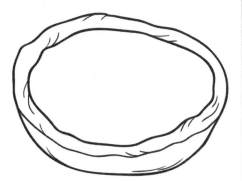

Deep Dish

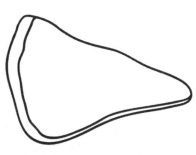

Thin and Crispy

Rectangular Crust

Math Objectives That Meet Standards

Children will:

1. Compare the number of objects (Chapter 2, Number Sense and Numeration).
2. Add and subtract whole numbers 1–10 using concrete objects (Chapter 3, Computation and Estimation).
3. Recognize, name, describe, compare, and make basic shapes (Chapter 5, Geometry and Spatial Sense).
4. Sort and classify materials by one or more attributes (Chapter 6, Sorting, Classifying, Graphing, Data Analysis, and Probability).
5. Select and apply a strategy to solve a problem (Chapter 8, Problem Solving and Reasoning).

How to Do It

○ On chart paper, write the names of different kinds of pizza crusts in large print. Glue pizza pictures next to the names of the crusts if the children cannot yet read the words.

○ Assemble a collection of different pizza crust pictures cut from newspapers, magazines, and from collateral sales pieces, like fliers and paper menus from pizza parlors.

○ During Group Time, display the chart.

○ Pass out several pizza pictures to the children.

○ Encourage the children to look at each picture and decide what kind of crust the picture shows.

○ Set out a glue stick, and have the children glue the images of the pizza types under the correct pizza crust names on the chart.

○ After they have finished gluing pizza pictures to the chart, ask the children to try doing some of the following:

  ○ Read the ads to find, and report on, the cost of each pizza.
  ○ Count the pictures in each pizza type; write the total for each group.
  ○ Think of another way to sort the pizza pictures (other than by type).
  ○ Graph the pizza-crust types.
  ○ Vote on the favorite pizza crust.

Double Crust

Take a Pizza Poll

Materials

paper on a clipboard and a pencil
newspaper and magazine picture ads
of pizzas with different toppings

In Addition

Pizza means *pie* in Italian. Pizzas
have been around for over 2,000
years. The first pizzas were topped
with olive oil and herbs; later,
vegetables were added. The
cornucopia of today's pizza toppings
expanded in America, with pizza
parlors trying to outdo each other.

Math Objectives That Meet Standards

Children will:

1. Understand that numbers represent the same quantity (Chapter 2, Number Sense and Numeration).
2. Use measurement vocabulary (greater than/less than/same as) (Chapter 4, Measurement, Time, and Money).
3. Gather data from familiar experiences by counting and tallying (Chapter 6, Sorting, Classifying, Graphing, Data Analysis, and Probability).
4. Make a step-by-step plan to solve a problem (Chapter 8, Problem Solving and Reasoning).

How to Do It

- Glue different pizza pictures down the left side of the sheet of paper on the clipboard.
- Draw lines across the length of the paper under each pizza picture (see the sample chart on appendix page 182).
- Give the clipboard to the class leader for the day and have her go around the room to show the pictures and ask the other children which pizzas they like the best. She tallies the results on the clipboard.

Pepperoni

Cheese

Sausage and Onion

Hamburger Meat

Peppers and Onion

Everything

Pizza Graph

Materials

grid drawn on chart paper
crayons
tally sheet from the previous
    activity, "Take a Pizza Poll"

Math Objectives That Meet Standards

Children will:
1. Use numbers to describe how many objects are in a set (Chapter 2, Number Sense and Numeration).
2. Interpret and use information from graphs to answer questions (Chapter 6, Sorting, Classifying, Graphing, Data Analysis, and Probability).
3. Recognize patterns to predict cause and effect (Chapter 7, Patterns and Number Relationships).
4. Organize information to answer the question or solve the problem (Chapter 8, Problem Solving and Reasoning).

How to Do It

- Make a graph of the best-liked pizzas. During Group Time, put up the tally sheet from "Take a Pizza Poll" on page 182.
- Have the children transfer the information to a grid like the one shown in the illustration on appendix page 183 and color the appropriate boxes to create a bar graph.
- Talk with the children about how both the tally sheet and the graph show the same information but in different forms.
- Explain that sometimes information is best shown in graph form and sometimes as a tally. There are other ways, too. Like with most things, there are many ways to show information. The best thing for the children to know is that they have options for how to try answering questions and solving problems. For instance, "How can I get the information I need to answer question X, and how can I present it so it will be understood easily?"

How Do You Make Pizza?

Materials

one piece of paper for each child
crayons or markers

Math Objectives That Meet Standards

Children will:
1. Understand and use a math vocabulary (Chapter 2, Number Sense and Numeration).
2. Combine and separate sets of objects to make new sets (Chapter 3, Computation and Estimation).
3. Sequence events by duration (Chapter 4, Measurement, Time, and Money).
4. Identify basic geometric shapes in the physical world (Chapter 5, Geometry and Spatial Sense).
5. Compare and contrast objects (Chapter 6, Sorting, Classifying, Graphing, Data Analysis, and Probability).
6. Recognize patterns in the physical world (Chapter 7, Patterns and Number Relationships).
7. Select and use appropriate mathematical tools (Chapter 8, Problem Solving and Reasoning).

In Addition

A famous pizzeria chef, Raffaele Esposito, was once asked to make a pizza for Queen Margarita of Italy (1851–1926). He added mozzarella cheese, tomatoes, and green basil to match the colors of the Italian flag. The original mozzarella cheese he used was made from water buffalo milk. There is no explanation, however, of how water buffalos were milked.

How to Do It

- This is a small group activity, best when done with three or four children at a time, while other children are in centers.
- Before reading any books about pizza or talking about how to make a pizza, give the children sheets of paper and markers or crayons and ask them to write their own recipes for pizza.
- If the children aren't ready to write, write their recipes for them.
- As the children name the ingredients, ask them how much or how many of each ingredient they want to include. Start with the crust and move upward through the sauces and the toppings.
- The children will give a variety of interesting responses to how to make a pizza. One of my favorites is "Visit Pizza Hut," a suggestion from Edward, one of my wittier four-year-olds. It was his attempt to solve a problem by having someone else do it.
- When all the recipes are completed, copy all the pages and put them together in several recipe books for the children to take home. The parents love the recipes. Some parents even used them for making pizzas (with some minor modifications).

What's on a Pizza Face?

Materials

Pizza Face by David Drew

Count on This

Young children have strong likes and dislikes. They are setting up boundaries that help them define who they are. That is why it is so important for young children to have choices and to make decisions. It is also important in helping to relieve their anxieties about experiences that they might not want to have, such as eating pizza they do not like. So make sure they know in advance what your expectations are, and discuss them fully with the children.

Math Objectives That Meet Standards

Children will:

1. Recognize numbers 1–10 and fractions ½, ¼ (Chapter 2, Number Sense and Numeration).
2. Add and subtract whole numbers 1–10 using concrete objects (Chapter 3, Computation and Estimation).
3. Understand the benefits of standard measurement (Chapter 4, Measurement, Time, and Money).
4. Identify shapes in the physical world (Chapter 5, Geometry and Spatial Sense).
5. Sort and classify real objects and pictures and explain how the sorting was done (Chapter 6, Sorting, Classifying, Graphing, Data Analysis, and Probability).
6. Make step-by-step plans to solve problems (Chapter 8, Problem Solving and Reasoning).

How to Do It

- Do this after the previous activity, "How Do You Make Pizza?" Compare recipes and talk about other pizza toppings.
- Ask the children how they might make a face with just the pizza toppings they like. During Group Time, share *Pizza Face* with the children. There is one sentence on each page, most of which contain a new ingredient or topping to add to make a pizza face.
- The recipe for pizza on the book's second page includes ingredients that many children don't like. They are relieved when, on Page 16, they are offered a chance to "Make a different pizza." For example, most children don't like olives, salami, onion, red pepper, and pineapple on their pizzas. They are overjoyed when they find out they are not going to have to eat the pizza from the book.

Felt Pizza?

Materials

felt, in different colors, to match the color of pizza ingredients (see illustrations on appendix page 184)

plastic baggies

pizza pan or a pizza serving box

cardboard circle that fits into the pan or box

multiple copies of a pizza order form (see illustration on appendix page 185)

basket

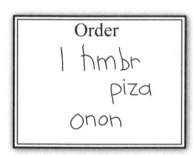

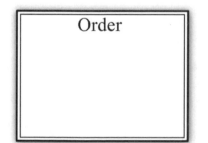

Math Objectives That Meet Standards

Children will:

1. Use numbers to describe the number of objects in sets and fractions ½ and ¼ (Chapter 2, Number Sense and Numeration).
2. Combine and separate sets of objects to make new sets (Chapter 3, Computation and Estimation).
3. Compare size, length, distance, and time (Chapter 4, Measurement, Time, and Money).
4. Identify basic geometric shapes in the physical world (Chapter 5, Geometry and Spatial Sense).
5. Sort and classify materials by one or more characteristics (Chapter 6, Sorting, Classifying, Graphing, Data Analysis, and Probability).
6. Select and apply strategies to solve problems (Chapter 8, Problem Solving and Reasoning).

How to Do It

○ Select the size of your pizza (which is the size of cardboard circle or pan you select for your pizza "crust").

○ Decide on the number of pieces you want of each topping and cut them out of the felt. Store the pieces in separate plastic storage bags.

○ The illustrations on appendix page 184 show typical pizza ingredients cut from felt. Cut out the following:
  ○ one piece for mushrooms,
  ○ two pieces for olives,
  ○ three peppers
  ○ four pieces for the tomato sauce,
  ○ five jalapeno peppers,
  ○ six pineapples slices,
  ○ seven onions,
  ○ eight hamburger pieces,
  ○ nine pepperoni slices, and
  ○ 10 cheese slices.

○ Write the number of pieces of each ingredient on the outside of the plastic bags in which they are stored.

○ Introduce the pizza with all the felt pieces during Group Time.

○ Encourage the children to come up and put a pizza together.

○ After they familiarize themselves with how to make the pizza, return the pieces to the baggies.

○ If appropriate, show the children a copy of an order form, like the illustration on appendix page 185, and illustrate to the children both how to place an order for a pizza, and how to copy down an order for a pizza.

- Use a child to model how to order the pizza, and afterwards, show everyone how the order form matches the order request the child made.
- Move the activity to the Math Center.
- Put a stack of order forms in a basket along with the felt pizza ingredients.
- Challenge the children to write orders and have other children complete the orders using the felt ingredients.
- To facilitate ordering, post a few sample orders on the wall nearby.
- Here is an easy order to fill:
  - Pizza with tomato sauce, one olive, two jalapenos, five pepperoni slices, and seven slices of cheese.
- Here are *harder* orders to fill:
  - Pizza with tomato sauce, with three olives on half of the pizza and five onions on the other half. Put 10 cheese slices on the whole pizza.
  - Pizza with tomato sauce, ¼ of the pizza with nine pepperoni slices, ¼ with two olives, ¼ with seven onion slices, and ¼ with eight hamburger pieces. Put 10 cheese slices on the whole pizza.

The Little Red Hen Makes a Pizza

Materials

The Little Red Hen Makes a Pizza by Philemon Sturges

In Addition

The largest pizza ever made had 45 pounds of cheese on the crust. It was 8' wide at the outer edge and almost 20' long. Bon appetite!

Math Objectives That Meet Standards

Children will:

1. Understand and use math vocabulary (Chapter 2, Number Sense and Numeration).
2. Use standard and nonstandard measurement (Chapter 4, Measurement, Time, and Money).
3. Find concrete objects in the environment that depict geometric shapes (Chapter 5, Geometry and Spatial Sense).
4. Reproduce patterns in sound and physical movement (Chapter 7, Patterns and Number Relationships).
5. Explain the reasonableness of solutions (Chapter 8, Problem Solving and Reasoning).

How to Do It

- Read *The Little Red Hen Makes a Pizza* during Group Time. Point out to the children that the book illustrations are made of collages of different geometric shapes.
- *The Little Red Hen* storyline is a familiar one, but in this variation: Little Red Hen makes the pizza dough, chops the ingredients, and bakes the pizza. In the end, Little Red Hen shares the pizza with the dog, the duck, and the cat, and they all wash the dishes.
- There are lots of pictures of pizza-making tools and toppings, as well as excellent points of discussion to keep the children engaged with the story.
- After you have read the story, ask the children to dramatize it using simple props in their retelling.

Pizza Party

Materials

pizza recipe written on a large chart on a stand

one half of an English muffin for each child

tomato sauce

grated mozzarella cheese

one slice of mozzarella cheese for each child

sliced pepperoni (popular but optional)

onions, bell peppers, Jalapenos, hamburger meat (optional)

two oven trays (for cooking the English-muffin pizzas)

access to an oven

Math Objectives That Meet Standards

Children will:

1. Use one-to-one correspondence (Chapter 2, Number Sense and Numeration).
2. Use numbers make predictions, estimates, and reasonable guesses (Chapter 3, Computation and Estimation).
3. Use non-standard measurement (Chapter 4, Measurement, Time, and Money).
4. Understand the benefits of using standard measurement (Chapter 4, Measurement, Time, and Money).
5. Tell time to the half-hour using an analog or digital clock (Chapter 4, Measurement, Time, and Money).
6. Describe and compare real-life objects to solid geometric shapes (Chapter 5, Geometry and Spatial Sense).
7. Compare and contrast objects (Chapter 6, Sorting, Classifying, Graphing, Data Analysis, and Probability).
8. Recognize patterns in the physical world (Chapter 7, Patterns and Number Relationships).
9. Make a step-by-step plan to solve problems (Chapter 8, Problem Solving and Reasoning).

How to Do It

- Make a small pizza for each child. Follow the recipe below:
  1. Put all the muffins on the trays, add a slice of mozzarella cheese to each muffin, and spread half a ladle of tomato sauce over the cheese. (**Note:** Adding the tomato sauce *after* the cheese keeps the muffin from getting soggy.)
  2. Add child-selected toppings as desired. Sprinkle a handful of grated cheese on top of the pizzas.
  3. Bake at 450° for about 20 minutes (or until the edges are brown and the cheese is bubbling).
- Before making the pizzas, prepare for a party by writing the pizza's recipe on a chart. Add pictures or advertisement photographs next to each ingredient or topping.
- Put the chart out of sight until you discuss how to make pizza with the children during Group Time.
- Write down some of the children's ideas about pizza making.
- After the children share their pizza-making thoughts, display the recipe chart, and read it with the children.
- After reading the chart, let the children eliminate or add any ingredients they want.
- When the children know how to make pizza and what they will use, ask them to help make a grocery list to shop for ingredients, and estimate how much money they will need to buy all of the ingredients. Their estimates will range from "about a dime" to "a million dollars."
- When you are ready for your pizza party, make the first pizza in front of the children, then move them into small groups of three or four and have them make pizzas together.

In Addition

- The number of ingredients used will be the biggest problem because the children will want to put more stuff on their pizzas than is possible.
- As the children make their pizzas, ask them questions: how much of a particular ingredient are they using, how many ingredients all together, how long will it take to cook the pizza?
- Have strips of aluminum foil handy for the children to put their names on, and put them under each pizza before you start.
- Bake all of the pizzas together, setting up different activities to do while the pizzas are cooling.
- Waiting to eat is always difficult, so while the children wait, read other pizza stories to them. Select from the list below. When the pizzas have cooled, have a party!

Pizza Tools

Materials

large tray
rolling pin
ladle
large spoon
baking pan
wooden paddle
pizza cutter
plastic knife
cutting board
cheese grater
ice-cream scoop

Math Objectives That Meet Standards

Children will:

1. Sort and classify real objects, and pictures of real objects, and explain how the sorting was done (Chapter 6, Sorting, Classifying, Graphing, Data Analysis, and Probability).

How to Do It

- During Group Time, put out a tray with several pizza-making tools for the children to see.
- Talk with the children about the tools that are and are not appropriate to use when making pizzas. For example, if you want to have pepperoni on your pizza, you need the plastic knife to cut the pepperoni. If you do not want grated cheese on your pizza, you would not need a cheese grater.
- Talk about what to do with each tool, and how each is used to make pizza.
- Have the children tell you which tools would not be necessary for them to make a pizza because they wouldn't use the ingredients that make those tools necessary. Let them explain why.
- Teach the children Pepperoni Pizza (below) as a chant, poem, or song. Use it often during your pizza unit.

Pepperoni Pizza by Sharon MacDonald
(from the *Watermelon Pie and Other Tunes!* CD by Sharon MacDonald)

Make mine pepperoni
Pizza, if you please.
Little sausage slices
In a pool of gooey cheese.

Make mine pepperoni.
Other pizza's fine.
You can eat all of yours,
And I'll eat all of mine.

And I don't care about pizza crust,
I'll take it thick or thin.
No, I don't care about the pizza crust,
If pepperoni's in.

So...Make mine pepperoni
Pizza, if you please.
Little sausage slices
In a pool of gooey cheese.

Make mine pepperoni.
Other pizza's fine.
You can eat all of yours,
Please don't ask for mine.

Yes, make mine pepperoni.
Other pizza's fine.
You eat all of yours,
But, the pepperoniiiiiiiiiiiiiiiiiiiiii's mine!

Glossary

Attribute—A quality an object or person has, such as color, shape, size, height, flavor, texture, or odor. Children learn to sort and classify by attributes.

Classifying—The process of grouping similar objects. To be able to classify, a child must recognize similar attributes or characteristics among various objects. For example, classifying socks with holes in the toes and those with no holes in the toes makes sense to young children.

Collage—An assembly of pieces of paper, fabric, or other materials usually glued to the surface of a heavy paper or board called a *base*.

Communication—The way in which children use math words to describe ideas. For example: *two, less, small, yesterday, long, first, more, at, same, in, square, far away, old, big, how many?, when?, time, day, faster, bunch,* and *measure*.

Computation—The process of solving mathematical problems using the rules of addition and subtraction. Young children start by counting concrete objects and matching them to a number. By using the rules of computation, children learn that a single operation, like subtraction, answers questions, such as, "If I have three cookies and I eat two of them, how many do I have left?"

Data analysis—The interpretation of accumulated information. For example, if the children want to discuss the most popular shoes in the class, they will need to collect data on all the different types of shoes everyone is wearing.

Estimation—The process of approximating, or guessing, based upon limited information. Estimates are subject to change, as more information about the subject becomes available.

Geometry—The study of geometric shapes, including the angles and proportions of the world around us. Shapes define our environment; they include the circle, triangle, square, rectangle, rhombus, and ellipse.

Graphing—Visually displaying the comparison between two or more objects. For example, the children might want to know what different kinds of shoes the children in the class are wearing. To find out, the children can take off their shoes, count the different kinds, and display their findings on a bar graph.

Interactive—Learning that occurs when children are involved directly in the activity for a hands-on experience.

Math—The process of calculating, understanding, and representing the relationships between numbers, events, objects, systems, and cycles, in an organized way.

Measurement—The process of determining the amount of something and giving it a number in units. This makes it possible to compare the number unit of one thing to the number units of others. Simply stated, measurement answers questions such as, "Is it more, or less, or the same?" Normally, measurements are taken in standard units like inches, but it is also possible to take measurements in non-standard units, like the length of a shoe.

Money—The way we pay for the things we want or need. It is a measurement of value. Children begin by learning to count money, and then they learn about what they can purchase with different amounts of money.

Number—A symbol for a unit of one or more things. Another word for number is *numeral*. The word *numeral* describes the symbolic version of a number. For example: "There were 11 people on the island" ("11" in this case is a numeral). However, when writing about numerals, they are called *numbers*. For example, "Eleven is the *number* of people on the island."

Number relationships—The inherent patterns in numbers.

Number sense—The awareness that numbers help us organize our day-to-day lives to accomplish the things we want to do.

Number sentence— A mathematical instruction in algebraic form, such as $2 + 3 = ?$ or $6 - 4 = ?$

Numeration—Another term for counting.

Numerical inclusion—Refers to the *total* number of something. For example, "five children" refers to the total number of children, but "fifth child" refers to one particular child.

Ordinal counting—Describes positions in a series (for example, fifth, tenth). During the day, when an activity arises in which objects or the children are in different ordinal positions, ask the children questions such as, "Which/Who came first? Second? Sixth?" "Who is the fifth person in line?" "What comes after first?" "What was the third little pig doing?"

Patterns—Sequences that repeat. The simplest patterns are ABAB and ABBABB. Patterns are all around us in the natural displays and configurations we see, like the sediment layers in an exposed hillside, or in the numbers we use. Often, the closer we look at a pattern, the more patterns we find.

Prediction—The act of determining what is likely to happen in a *future event or problem* based on current observations. Estimates, on the other hand, attempt to provide an answer to a problem that exists.

Probability—The likelihood that an event will or will not occur. For example, what is the probability that most of the children will wear the same shoes tomorrow?

Problem solving—Finding solutions and posing questions. Young children come to problem solving easily because they are naturally curious and enthusiastic about new experiences.

Rational counting—The process of matching, in order, each number name to a series of objects in a group.

Reasoning—When children draw conclusions from a given set of facts or circumstances, when they can explain events and the methods used to compile and communicate information. Reasoning means thinking, explaining one's thoughts, and coming up with a plan. Reasoning is a systematic, flexible approach to problem solving. It is a learned behavior.

Rotation symmetry—The rotation around an axis, such as in a tricycle wheel that spins.

Rote counting—Reciting the order of numbers from memory: "1, 2, 3, 4, 5, 6, 7, 8, 9, 10."

Seriation—The arrangement of objects in a series by some prescribed criteria, such as size, shape, color, weight, length, or texture. To seriate by size, for example, a child puts objects in order from smallest to largest or largest to smallest. To seriate by distance, a more abstract measurement, ask, "Which house is farthest away?" "Which is the next farthest away?" "Which is closest?" To seriate by volume, for example, to compare the amount of liquid in several jars, ask, "Which jar is fullest?"

Sorting—Separating items by their similarities and differences. The simplest form of sorting is **matching**.

Spatial sense—An awareness of one's relationship to other things in terms of *position* ("Where am I?"), *direction* ("Which way do I go?") and *distance* ("How far away/near am I?"). Spatial sense also involves organizing space so things fit appropriately for work and play, or organizing objects to please the eye. Spatial-sense organization requires children to recognize patterns and duplicate and extend patterns.

Subtraction—The process of deducting one number from another number—you end up with less than you had when you started.

Symmetry—Balance to the mind and to the eye.

Time—Standard units that measure one moment to another.

Appendix

Building Block Cards

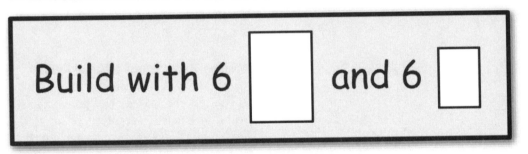

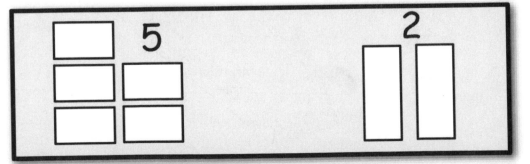

How to Build a Math Stand

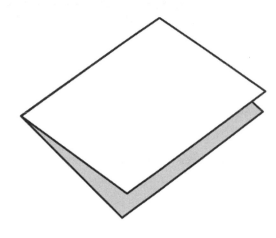

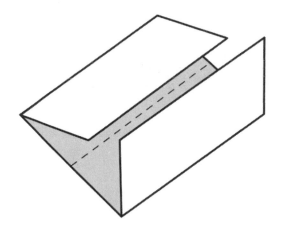

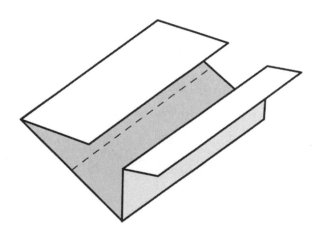

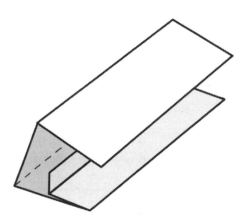

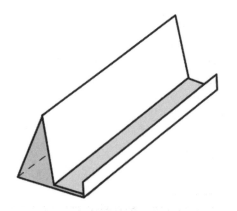

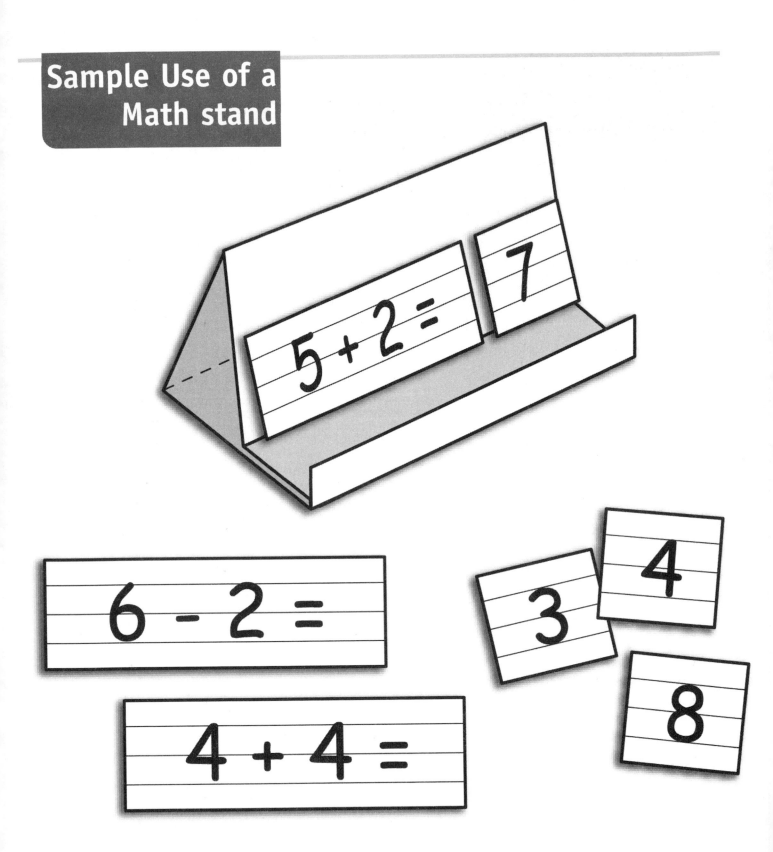

Outdoor Thermometer

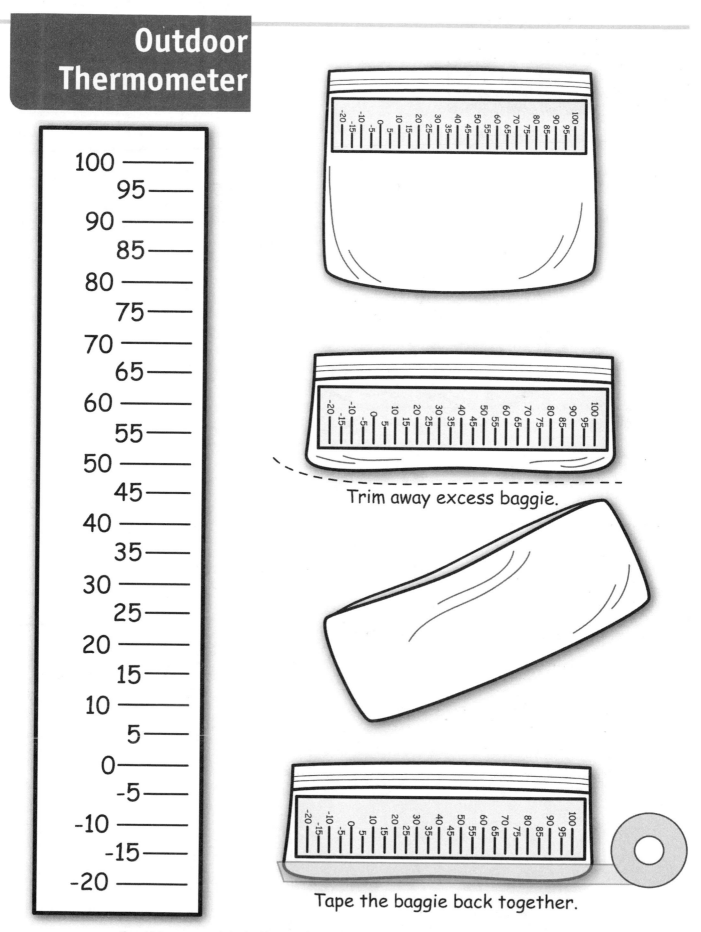

Trim away excess baggie.

Tape the baggie back together.

Coin and Dollar Illustrations

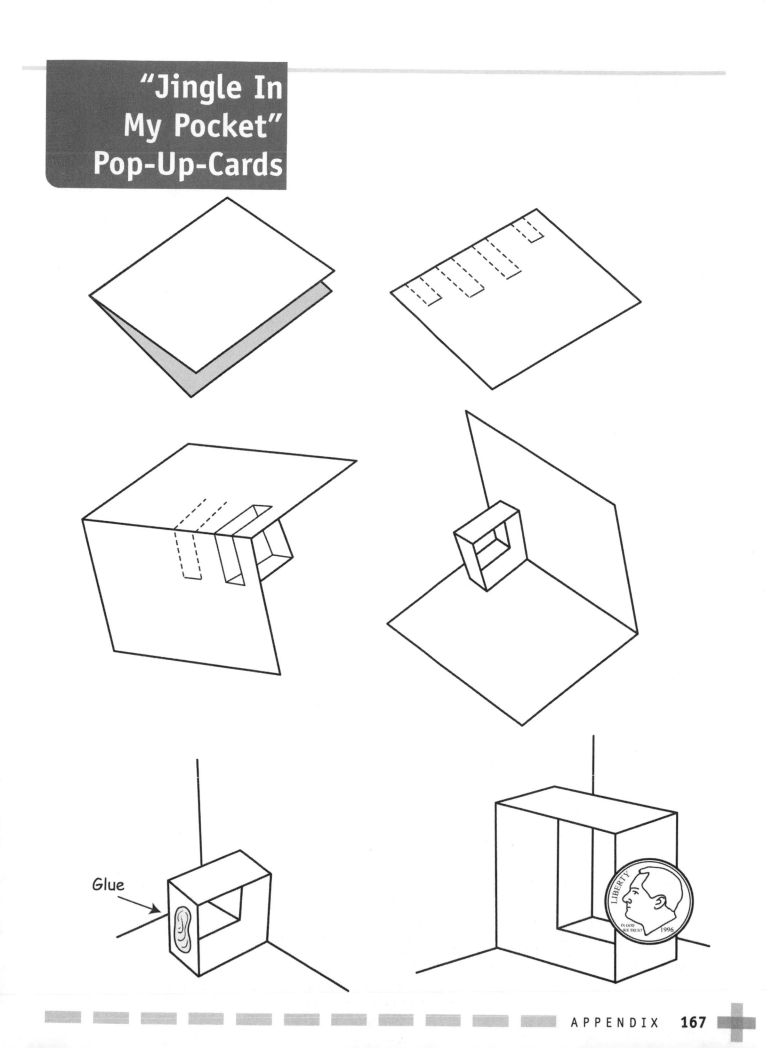

"Jingle In My Pocket" Pop-Up-Cards

Glue

Unit Block Silhouettes

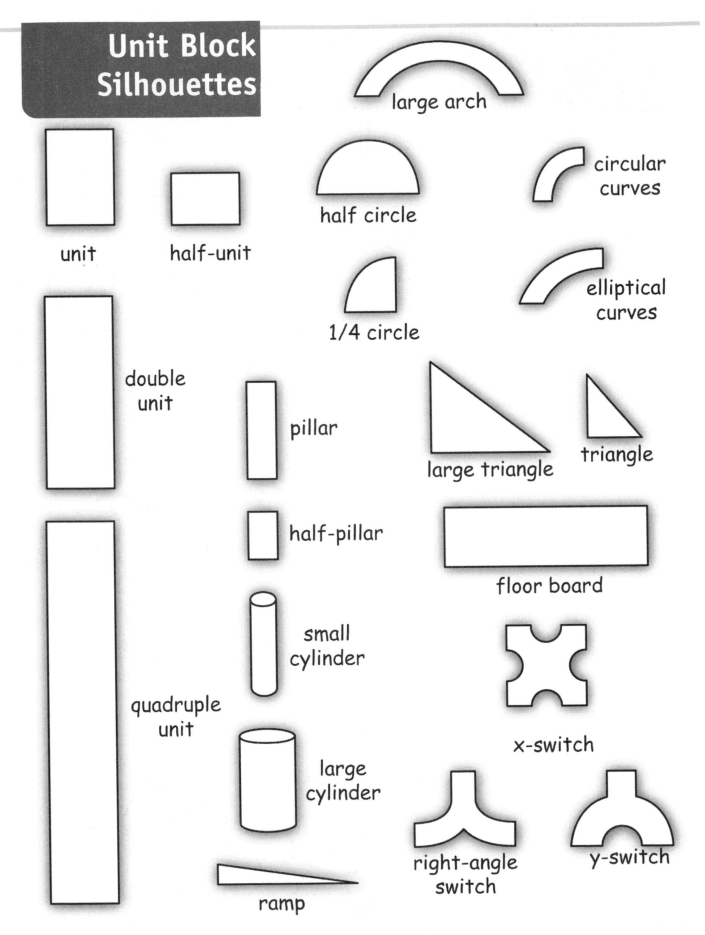

large arch

unit

half-unit

half circle

circular curves

1/4 circle

elliptical curves

double unit

pillar

large triangle

triangle

half-pillar

floor board

small cylinder

x-switch

quadruple unit

large cylinder

right-angle switch

y-switch

ramp

CD Geometry-Sample Figures

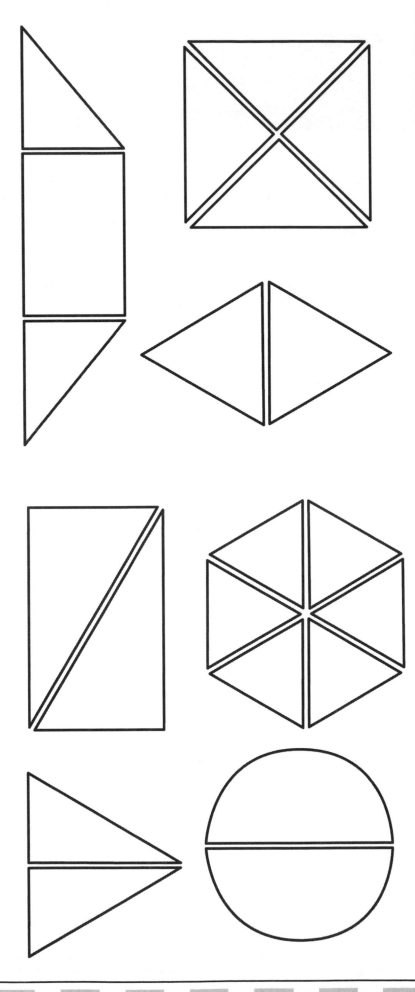

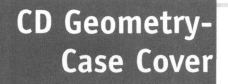

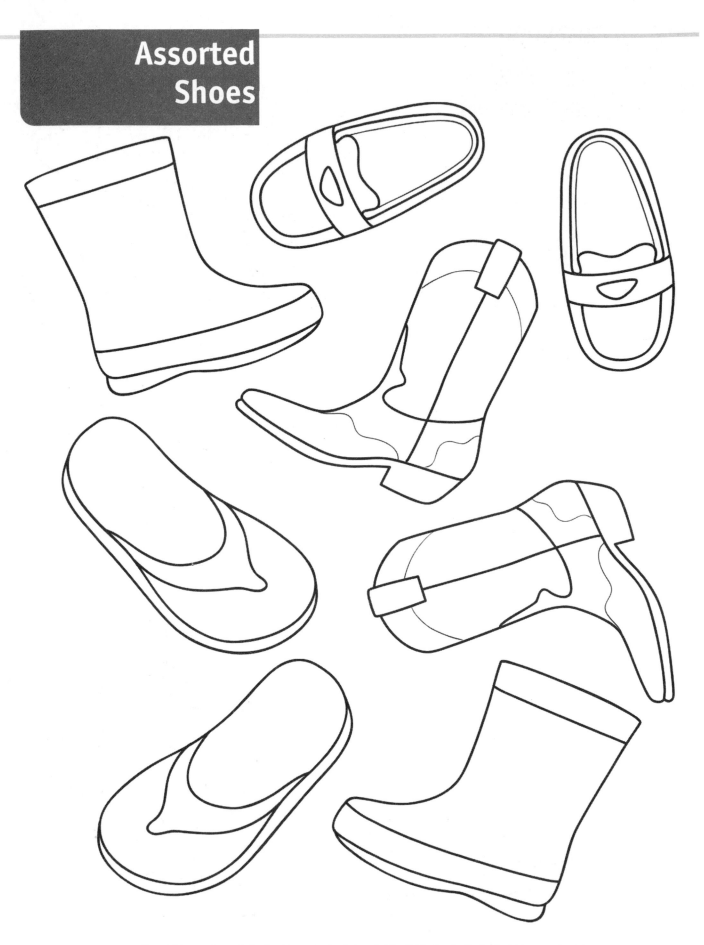

Assorted Shoes

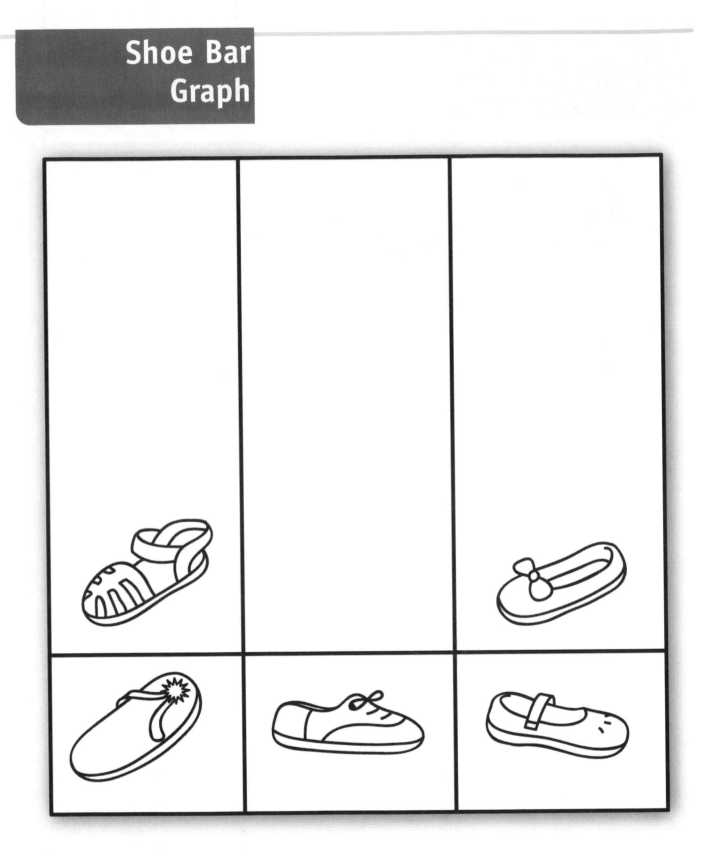

Crayon Color Bar Graph

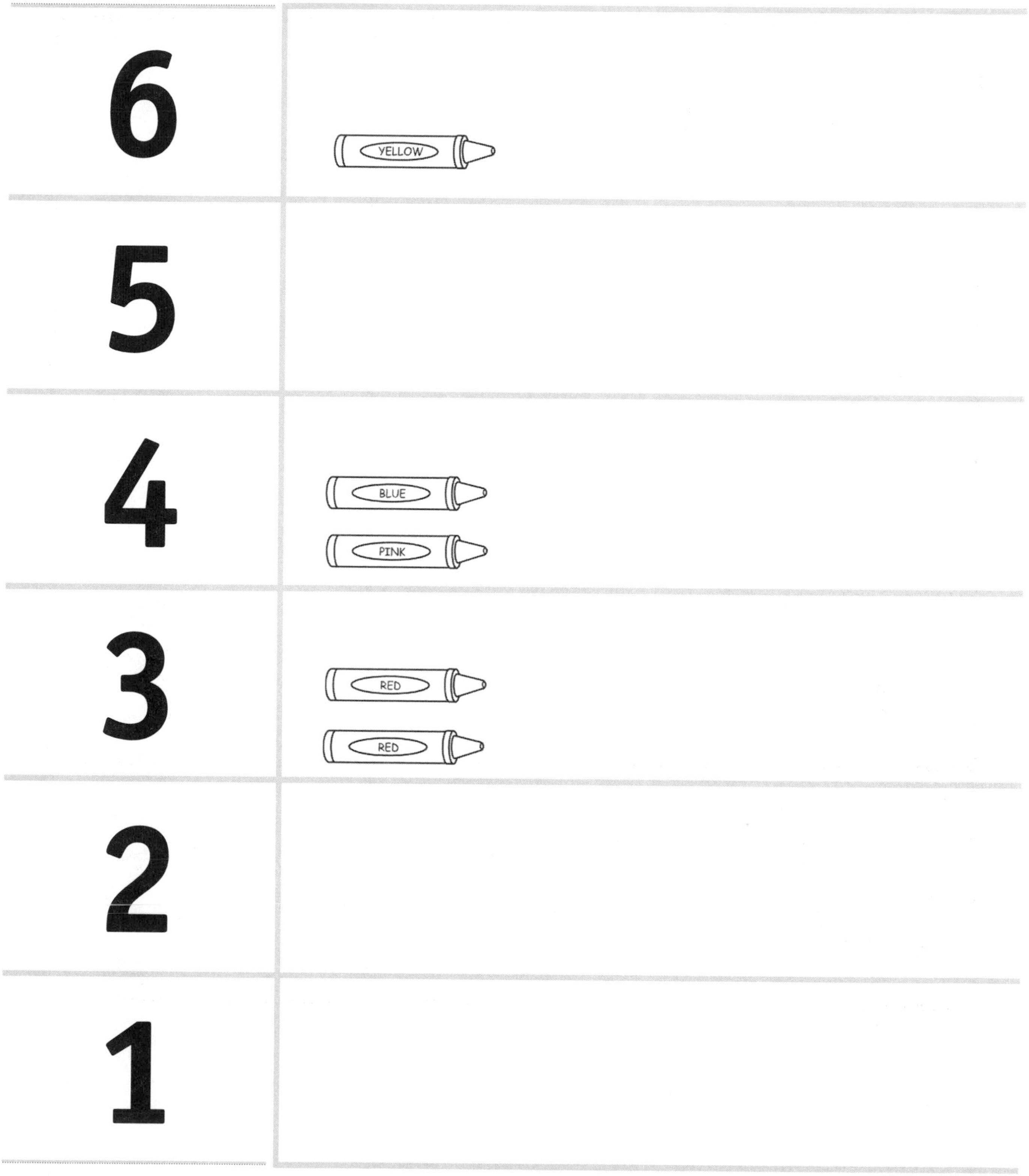

6

YELLOW

5

4

BLUE

PINK

3

RED

RED

2

1

Weather Graph

Key
Sunny = yellow
Rainy = blue
Cloudy = black
Icy (Snowy) = light blue

Total Days

Sunny

Windy

Rainy

Cloudy

Cold

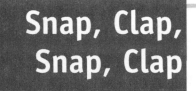
Snap, Clap, Snap, Clap

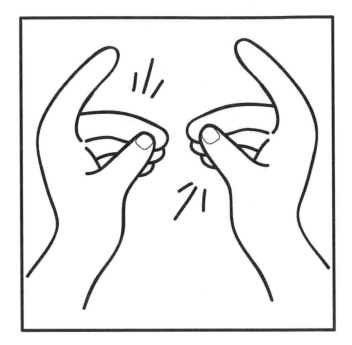

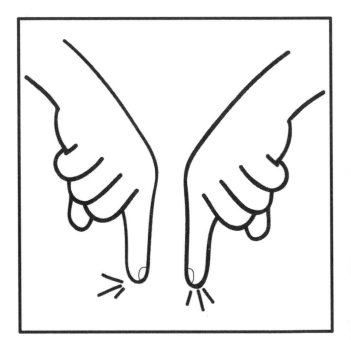

Make the apple whole!

Make the apple whole!

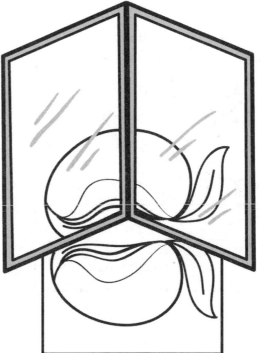

Pizza Poll

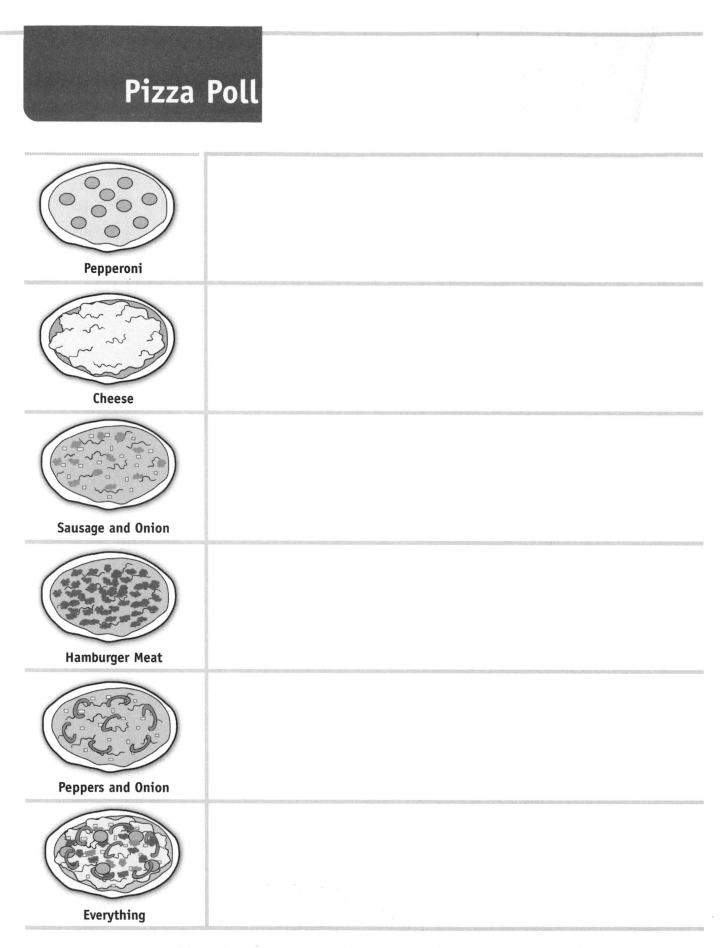

Pepperoni

Cheese

Sausage and Onion

Hamburger Meat

Peppers and Onion

Everything

Pizza Graph

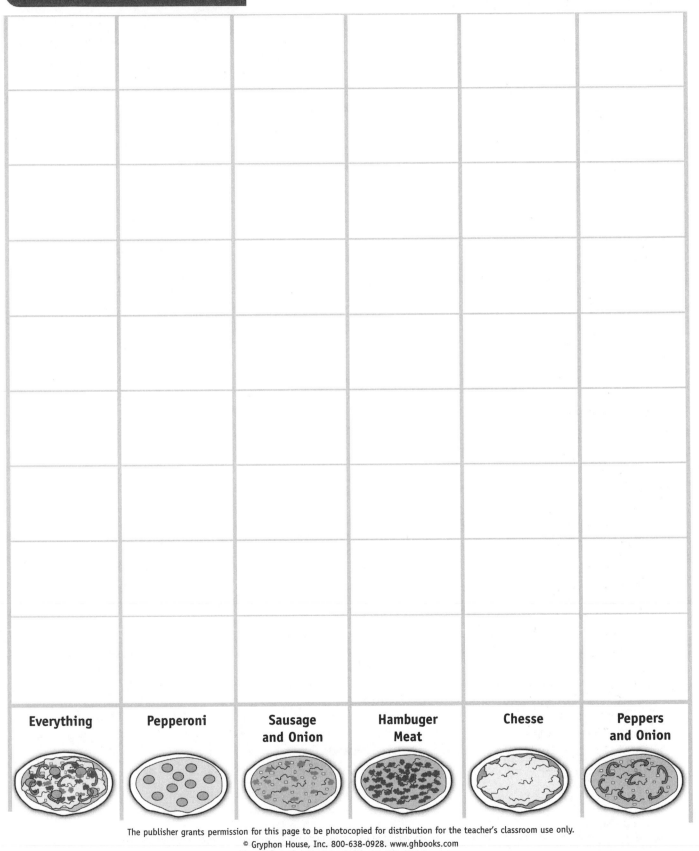

Everything	Pepperoni	Sausage and Onion	Hambuger Meat	Chesse	Peppers and Onion

Pizza Ingredients

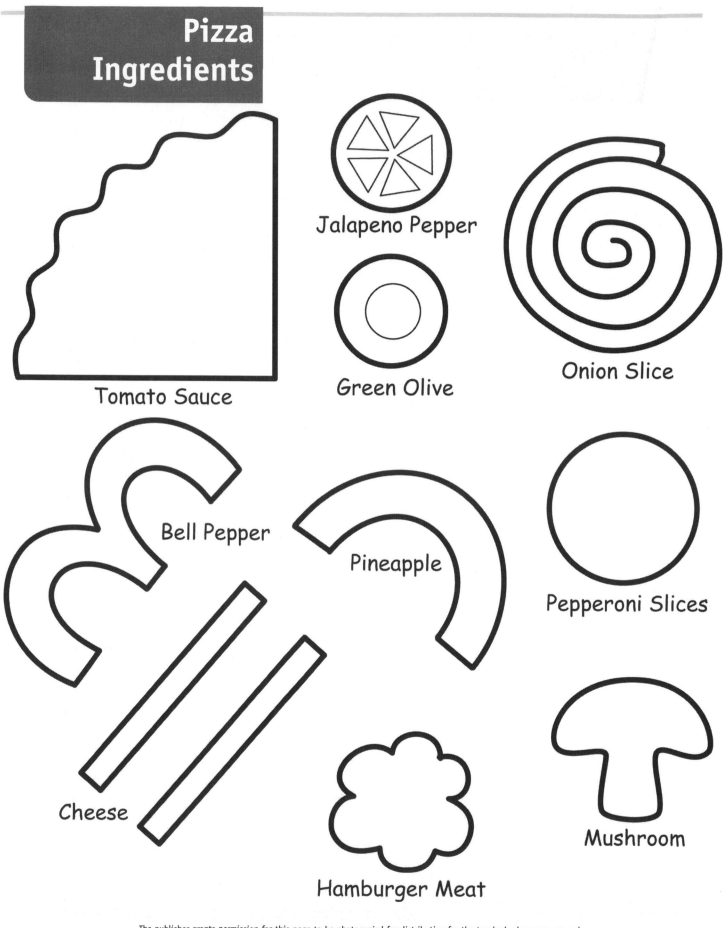

Tomato Sauce

Jalapeno Pepper

Green Olive

Onion Slice

Bell Pepper

Pineapple

Pepperoni Slices

Cheese

Hamburger Meat

Mushroom

Order

I hmbr

piza

onon

Order

I chese

pizza

Order

NCTM Standards

1. Numbers and Operations

Children will:

A. Understand numbers, ways of representing numbers, relationships among numbers, and number systems.

B. Understand meanings of operations and how they relate one another.

C. Compute fluently and make reasonable estimates.

2. Algebra

Children will:

A. Understand patterns, relations, and functions.

B. Represent and analyze mathematical situations and structures using algebraic symbols.

C. Use mathematical models to represent and understand quantitative relationships.

D. Analyze changes in various contexts.

3. Measurement

Children will:

A. Understand measurable attributes of objects and the units, systems, and processes of measurement.

B. Apply appropriate techniques, tools, and formulas to determine measurements.

4. Geometry

Children will:

A. Analyze characteristics and properties of two- and three-dimensional geometric shapes and develop mathematical arguments about geometric relationships.

B. Specify locations and describe spatial relationships using coordinate geometry and other representational systems.

C. Apply transformations and use symmetry to analyze mathematical situations.

D. Use visualization, spatial reasoning, and geometric modeling to solve problems.

5. Data Analysis and Probability

Children will:

A. Formulate questions that can be addressed with data, and collect, organize, and display relevant data to answer them.

B. Select and use appropriate statistical methods to analyze data.

C. Develop and evaluate inferences and predictions that are based on data.

D. Understand and apply basic concepts of probability.

6. Problem Solving Standards

Children will:

A. Build new mathematical knowledge through problem solving.

B. Solve problems that arise in mathematics and in other contexts.

C. Apply and adapt a variety of appropriate strategies to solve problems.

D. Monitor and reflect on the process of mathematical problem solving.

7. Representation

Children will:

A. Create and use representations to organize, record, and communicate mathematical ideas.

B. Select, apply, and translate among mathematical representations to solve problems.

C. Use representations to model and interpret physical, social, and mathematical phenomena.

8. Communication

Children will:

A. Organize and consolidate mathematical thinking through communication.

B. Communicate mathematical thinking coherently and clearly to peers, teachers, and others.

C. Analyze and evaluate the mathematical thinking and strategies of others.

D. Use the language of mathematics to express mathematical ideas precisely.

9. Reasoning and Proof

Children will:

A. Recognize reasoning and proof as fundamental aspects of mathematics.

B. Make and investigate mathematical conjectures.

C. Develop and evaluate mathematical arguments and proofs.

D. Select and use various types of reasoning and methods of proof.

Matrix of NCTM Standards and Activities

Chapter 2
Number Sense and Numeration

	NCTM Standards								
	1 Numbers and Operations	2 Algebra	3 Measurement	4 Geometry	5 Data Analysis and Probability	6 Problem Solving Standards	7 Representation	8 Communication	9 Reasoning and Proof
"Leaves Are Falling"	AB	AB		C					
"Leaves Are Falling" Interactive Chart	AB	AB							
Number Bag	A	AB							
Numeral/Number Bag Match	AB	AB							
Calendar Collage	A								
Number Rings	ABC	B							
Balloon Launch	A								
Number Bracelets	AC	AB	A	C					
I Spy Numbers Book	C	A							
Number Bottle	AC	B							
Before-and-After Calendar Days	BC								
Pompom Counting	A	AB							
Pompom-Dot Match	A	AB							
Pompom Toss	A	AB							
The Apple Thief	AC	B							
Block Cleanup Cards	AC	A							
Number Playing Cards	AC								
Coat Hanger Numbers	A	B							
Missing Numbers	ABC								
Card Game	ABC								
Ordinal Counting	C	B							
"Ely and The Five Little Piglets"	C	B							

CHAPTER 3
Computation and Estimation

NCTM Standards

Activity	1 Numbers and Operations	2 Algebra	3 Measurement	4 Geometry	5 Data Analysis and Probability	6 Problem Solving Standards	7 Representation	8 Communication	9 Reasoning and Proof
Activities That Teach Computation									
Adding Beads	ABC	C				C	B	D	
Button Spill	BC	BC			B		B		
Adding Domino Dots	ABC	C					B		
Adding a Die-Inside-a-Die	AB	BC							
12 Ways to Get to 11	A	A			A	A		ABC	A
Finger Ring Addition	ABC							A	
Lunch Bag Number Book	ABC	C							
Addition on Fold-Out Flaps	ABC					A		B	
Block Building Cards	ABC	C							
Library Pocket Math	ABC	D							
Number Sentence Bracelet	ABC	AD			BC				
Adding Using Playing Cards	ABC	D							
License Plate Match	ABC								
"Five Round Pumpkins"	ABC								
Activities That Teach Estimation									
Model Estimation Station	AC								
Estimation Station Ideas	A	ACD			ABCD	C	B	ABC	AB
Estimation Station	C	A			ACD	D	B	C	
Throughout-the-Day Estimates	AC				BCD	AD		B	
Pompom Grab	AC				BCD	AD		BC	D
Estimation Jar or Box	AC	A							

NCTM Standards

Activity	1 Numbers and Operations	2 Algebra	3 Measurement	4 Geometry	5 Data Analysis and Probabilty	6 Problem Solving Standards	7 Representation	8 Communication	9 Reasoning and Proof
Activities That Teach Measurement									
Tape Measure	B		AB					D	
Daily Temperature		D	AB				A	D	
Track the Weather		D	AB				A	D	
Kitchen Scale	A		AB		AD				B
Charting Children's Weights	A	C	AB		C		A		
Measuring Children's Heights	A	C	AB		C		A		
Measuring with Pompoms			AB			AB			B
Activities That Teach Seriation									
Seriate Paint Color Sample Cards		AD	AB		AD	C			
Pompom Seriation		AD	AB		AD	C			
Activities That Teach About Time									
The In-One-Minute List	C		AB					D	D
Using a Timer to Time Events	A	D	AB		CD			B	
Timeline of Important School Events	A		AB			BC			
Announcement Clock	A	D	AB		AD	AB	C		
Schedule of Daily Events	A	D	AB		D		C	D	
Alarm Clock Time	AC		AB			B			
The "What Happens Over Time?" Book	A	A	AB		A			AB	
Appointment Book	A	A	AB		A		A	ABD	
The Wake-Up Chart	A	D	AB						

CHAPTER 4
Measurement, Money, and Time

NCTM Standards

Activities That Teach About Money	1 Numbers and Operations	2 Algebra	3 Measurement	4 Geometry	5 Data Analysis and Probability	6 Problem Solving Standards	7 Representation	8 Communication	9 Reasoning and Proof
100-Day Celebration	AB		AB	D	AB	C		B	
Penny-Date Progression Card	A	A	AB		A	A		A	
"Jingle in My Pocket"	AB		AB					A	
"Jingle in My Pocket" Chart	AB		AB				B		
"Jingle in My Pocket" Pop-Up Cards	AB		AB						
Piggy Bank Coin Counting	AB		AB			AB			
Coin Puzzles	AB		AB					D	
Hunt, Count, and Buy	AB		AB			D			
Coins Around the World	AB		AB						
Coin Date Line	AB		AB		A	B	B		

CHAPTER 5
Geometry and Spatial Sense

NCTM Standards

Activities That Teach Basic Shapes	1 Numbers and Operations	2 Algebra	3 Measurement	4 Geometry	5 Data Analysis and Probability	6 Problem Solving Standards	7 Representation	8 Communication	9 Reasoning and Proof
Geometric Shape Hunting		A		AD	A			AB	
Name That Unit Block!		A		ABD					
Gel Geometry				ABCD					
Spongy Geometry		AD		CD	C				
Painting on Shapes				ACD		A			
What's the Shape?		A		ACD		C	A		

NCTM Standards

Activity	1 Numbers and Operations	2 Algebra	3 Measurement	4 Geometry	5 Data Analysis and Probability	6 Problem Solving Standards	7 Representation	8 Communication	9 Reasoning and Proof
Rubbings of Shapes				ABCD	D				
Feeling Shapes in a Bag		A		ACD			C	D	
CD Case Geometry		A		ABCD			A	A	
Geometric Shapes in Architecture		AC		ABCD	A	B			
Neighborhood Walk		D		ABCD	A		C		
Neighborhood Walk Tab Book		A		ABCD		AD	AC		
Shapes in the Neighborhood		A		ABCD			B		
What Shapes Do You See?		A		ABCD					
The "I Spy Shapes" Game		A		ABCD				BD	
How to Eat Geometry		AD		ABCD					
Cookie Cutter Shapes		AD		ABCD			A		
Straw-and-Pipe-Cleaner Shapes		AD		ABCD			A		
Making Playing Card Suits		AD		ABCD				AD	
Geoboards		AD		ABCD			A		
Frame-a-Shape Game		AD		ABCD					A
Activities That Teach Spatial Sense									
Build in a Box		D		ABCD	A		C		
Classroom Photograph Puzzle		D		ABCD			C		
"Up and Down"		A		B				D	
Geometric Words in Block Construction		A		B				D	
Obstacle Course		A		B				D	
Doll Furniture in Block Center		A		ABCD			B		
Where Are You?		A		B				AD	
"Shuffle, Bend, Slide, and Wave"		A		B				AD	

CHAPTER 6

Graphing, Statistics, and Probability

NCTM Standards

Activities That Teach Sorting, Classifying, Graphing, Data Analysis, and Probability	1 Numbers and Operations	2 Algebra	3 Measurement	4 Geometry	5 Data Analysis and Probability	6 Problem Solving Standards	7 Representation	8 Communication	9 Reasoning and Proof
What Shoes Do You Choose?					ABCD		BC	ABD	D
"A Barefoot Walker's Shoes"					ABCD			ABD	
The Mixed-Up Pompom Sort					ABCD	AD		AC	
The Button Box					ABCD	AC		ABCD	BD
Button Graph					ABCD	C	ABC	ABD	ABD
Crayon Color Bar Graph					ABCD	C	ABC	ABD	ABD
Weather Graph					ABCD	C	ABC	ABD	ABD
Whole Body Graph					ABCD	C	ABC	ABD	ABD
Photo Graphs					ABCD	C	ABC	ABD	ABD
Cube-Me Graph					ABCD	C	ABC	ABD	ABD
Bag a Graph					ABCD	C	ABC	ABD	ABD
Yes-and-No Graph Bag					ABCD	C	ABC	ABD	ABD
A Year of Graphs					ABCD	C	ABC	ABD	BD
Venn Diagram Shoe Sort			A		ABCD	ABCD	ABC	ABD	BD
Coin Flip Tally					ABCD	AC	ABC	ABCD	ABD
Jug Tally					ABCD	AC	ABC	ABCD	ABD

CHAPTER 7
Patterns and Number Relationships

NCTM Standards

Activities That Teach Patterning Skills and Number Relationships	1 Numbers and Operations	2 Algebra	3 Measurement	4 Geometry	5 Data Analysis and Probability	6 Problem Solving Standards	7 Representation	8 Communication	9 Reasoning and Proof
Snap, Clap, Snap, Clap	A	ACD			C			B	
Boy, Girl, Boy, Girl Pattern Game	A	ACD			D	A		A	
Outside Patterns	A	ACD		A	AD			D	
Inside Patterns	A	ACD		A	AD			D	
Calendar Patterns	A	ABCD			ACD		B	AB	
Patterns on a Geoboard	A	ACD		B	A	ACD		D	
Block Pattern Cards	A	ACD		B	A	ACD		D	
Complete-the-Pattern Game	A	ACD		B	ACD	ACD		D	
Playing Card Pattern Game	A	ACD		B	A	ACD		ABD	
Photograph Patterns	A	ACD		B	A	ACD		ABC	
Patterns with Buttons	A	ACD		B	A	ACD		D	
Patterns with Pompoms	A	ACD		B	A	ACD		D	
"Cup Tapping" Patterns	A	ACD		B	A	ACD		ABCD	
Symmetry and Blocks	A	ACD		ABCD		ACD			
Symmetry and Mylar Mirrors	A	ACD		ABCD		ACD			
String Painting Symmetry	A	ACD		ABCD		ACD			
Symmetry Puzzle	A	ACD		ABCD		ACD			
Reflections on Symmetry	A	ACD		ABCD		ACD	AB	ABCD	

CHAPTER 8
Problem Solving and Reasoning

NCTM Standards

	1 Numbers and Operations	2 Algebra	3 Measurement	4 Geometry	5 Data Analysis and Probability	6 Problem Solving Standards	7 Representation	8 Communication	9 Reasoning and Proof
Activities That Teach Problem Solving and Reasoning									
The Little Plant That Could	AB		AB			ABCD			ABCD
How Many for Lunch?	AB		AB			ABCD			ABCD
How Do You Make a Jelly Sandwich with One Slice of Bread?	AB		AB			ABCD			ABCD
Where Is Sarah?	AB		AB			ABCD			ABCD
How Many Swings Make One Turn?	AB		AB			ABCD	ABC		ABCD
How Many Cans and Boxes?	AB		AB			ABCD			ABCD
What's Near? What's Far?	AB		AB			ABCD	ABC		ABCD
How Many Days Until Thanksgiving?	AB		AB			ABCD			ABCD

CHAPTER 9
Putting It All Together with Pizza

NCTM Standards

	1 Numbers and Operations	2 Algebra	3 Measurement	4 Geometry	5 Data Analysis and Probability	6 Problem Solving Standards	7 Representation	8 Communication	9 Reasoning and Proof
"Five Round Pizzas"	AB	A			A	A	AB	BD	CD
Pizza Crusts		AC		A	B	B	A	C	BCD
Take a Pizza Poll	AB	CD	A		ABCD	ACD			
Pizza Graph	AB	C			ABCD	ACD			
How Do You Make Pizza?	ABC		AB		ABCD		A	AB	
What's on a Pizza Face?	ABC		AB		ABCD				
Felt Pizza?	ABC		AB	A	ABCD	ABCD	B	ABD	B
The Little Red Hen Makes a Pizza	ABC		AB		ABCD				
Pizza Party	ABC		AB	A	ABCD	ABCD	B	ABD	B
Pizza Tools		AD		A	ABCD	A	A	A	

Math Books for Children

1 Hunter by Pat Hutchins—counting

12 Ways to Get to 11 by Eve Merriam—combinations

26 Letters and 99 Cents by Tana Hoban—money

365 Penguins by Jean-Luc Fromenthal—counting

Amelia's Road by Linda Jacobs Altman—attributes and classification

Anno's Counting Book by Mitsumasa Anno—counting

Architecture Counts by Michael J. Crosbie and Stephan Rosenthal—
geometry

Arlene Alda's 1 2 3 by Arlene Alda—number recognition

Baby Rattlesnake by Te Ata—measurement

Bears in Pairs by Niki Yektai—pairs

Benjamin's 365 Birthdays by Judi Barrett—time: day in year

Benny's Pennies by Pat Brisson—computation and money

Beware of Boys by Tony Blundell—problem solving

Bunches and Bunches of Bunnies by Louise Mathews—
multiplication/division

Bunny Money by Rosemary Wells—money

The Button Box by Margarette S. Reid—sorting/classifying

Clocks and More Clocks by Pat Hutchins—time

The Coin Counting Book by Rozanne Lanczak Williams—counting

Cookie Count by Robert Sabuda—counting

Count on Your Fingers African Style by Claudia Zaslavsky—
finger counting

The Crayon Counting Book by Pam Munoz Ryan and Jerry Pallotta—
counting by 2s (odd and even)

Domino Addition by Lynette Long—addition

Duckie's Ducklings by Frances Barry—counting

Each Orange Had 8 Slices by Paul Giganti—addition

Eating Fractions by Bruce McMillan—part/whole

Eggs for Tea by Jan Pienkowski—counting backwards

The Doorbell Rang by Pat Hutchins—dozen

The Dot and the Line by Norton Juster—geometry

The Father Who Had 10 Children by Benedicte Guettier—counting
to 10

The Giant's Toe by Brock Cole—measurement and estimation

The Great Pet Sale by Mick Inkpen—money

The Grouchy Ladybug by Eric Carle—time

How Big Is a Foot? by Rolf Myller—measurement

Inch by Inch by Leo Lionni—measurement

Jelly Beans for Sale by Bruce McMillan—money

Just a Minute! by Yuyi Morales—counting

Just Enough Carrots by Stuart J. Murphy—measurement

Let's Count by Tana Hoban—1 to 100

The Little Red Hen Makes a Pizza by Philemon Sturges—measurement

M&M Counting Book by Barbara Barbieri McGrath—counting

Make a Pizza Face by David Drew—sequence of step-by-step plan

Math Curse by Jon Scieszka—problem solving

Miss Bindergarten Celebrates the 100th Day of Kindergarten by Joseph
Slate—counting

More or Less a Mess by Shelia Keenan—sorting
The Mouse and the Apple by Stephen Butler—one-to-one
   correspondence
Much Bigger Than Martin by Steven Kellogg—size
Museum Shapes by The (NY) Metropolitan Museum of Art—patterns
One Fish Two Fish Red Fish Blue Fish by Dr. Seuss—counting
One Some Many by Marthe Jocelyn and Tom Slaughter—measurement
Ovals by Jennifer Burke—geometry: shapes
Over in the Meadow by Olive A. Wadsworth—counting
Over Under by Marthe Jocelyn and Tom Slaughter—measurement;
   spatial sense
The Patchwork Quilt by Valerie Flournoy—patterns
Pattern Bugs by Trudy Harris—patterns
Pigs Will Be Pigs by Amy Axelrod—money
Rectangles by Jennifer Burke—geometry: shapes
Shoes from Grandpa by Mem Fox—numeration
Spunky Monkeys on Parade by Stuart J. Murphy—skip counting
Squares by Jennifer Burke—geometry: shapes
Stars by Jennifer Burke—geometry: shapes
Ten, Nine, Eight by Molly Bang—patterns
Tortillas and Lullabies/Tortillas y cancioncitas by Lynn Reiser and
   Valientes Corazones—shapes
Two of Everything by Lily Toy Hong—pairs
Two Ways to Count to Ten by Ruby Dee—counting by 2s
What Is Square? by Rebecca Kai Dotlich—geometry: shapes
Who Sank the Boat? by Pamela Allen—measurement and seriation
Yertle the Turtle and Other Stories by Dr. Seuss—measurement

Math Websites for Teachers

www.journal.naeyc.org/btj
www.nctm.org
www.standards.nctm.org
www.mathperspectives.com
www.k111.k12.il.us/king/math.htm
http://pbskids.org/cyberchase/games
www.kidzone.ws/math
http://home.att.net/-cinetwork/math.htm
http://countdown/luc.edu
www.sharonmacdonald.com
www.drjean.org
www.rainbowsymphony.com
www.officeplayground.com
www.headstartinfo.org
www.mathforum.org
www.pfot.com

Index

Index

Everyday Discoveries
Amazingly Easy Science and Math Using Stuff You Already Have
Sharon MacDonald

Science and math concepts are embedded in the things children do every day. With this book, children learn the how, the why, and the what happens next with open-ended, self-directed activities. *Everyday Discoveries* shows how easily and naturally children can learn science and math in preschool programs, early primary classrooms, child care centers, and home care settings. 245 pages. 1998.

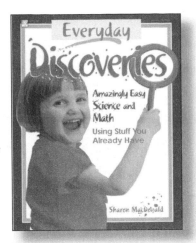

ISBN 978-0-87659-196-9 | PB | 18117

Block Play
The Complete Guide to Learning and Playing with Blocks
Sharon MacDonald

Create craft-board trees, railroad tracks, and skyscrapers, and watch children experience the joy of learning with blocks! Each activity includes clear descriptions of what children learn and encourages developmental skills such as problem-solving, math, science, language, and social skills. *Block Play* is a must-have for every teacher. 192 pages. 2001.

ISBN 978-0-87659-253-1 | PB | 19327

Sanity Savers for Early Childhood Teachers
200 Quick Fixes for Everything from Big Messes to Small Budgets
Sharon MacDonald

From clean-up solutions and storage ideas to inventive cost-cutting strategies, plus everything in between, this book will truly help you keep your sanity in the classroom! Use the creative suggestions to help children resolve conflicts and solve problems, to deal with interruptions in the classroom, and to utilize your classroom space effectively. *Sanity Savers* helps solve everyday problems, giving you more time to teach and enjoy the children in your classroom. 160 pages. 2004.

ISBN 978-0-87659-236-1 | PB | 16294